Essay Index

DATE DUE

FOUR
IN
AMERICA

FOUR
IN
AMERICA

GERTRUDE STEIN
INTRODUCTION BY THORNTON WILDER

Essay Index

Essay Index Reprint Series

BOOKS FOR LIBRARIES PRESS
FREEPORT, NEW YORK

ACKNOWLEDGMENT

The portion of "George Washington" entitled "Scenery and George Washington" is reprinted by permission of *Hound & Horn*.

STANDARD BOOK NUMBER:
8369-1381-7

LIBRARY OF CONGRESS CATALOG CARD NUMBER:
79-99650

PRINTED IN THE UNITED STATES OF AMERICA

CONTENTS

A NOTE ON THE MANUSCRIPT

Four in America was begun at Bilignin in 1932 and finished in Paris in 1933, the first long work to which Miss Stein turned her attention after she had finished writing *The Autobiography of Alice B. Toklas.* The section entitled "Scenery and George Washington" had been composed as a separate descriptive study probably as early as the autumn of 1931, and had already been printed at the time of its incorporation in the present work.

This text is based upon the typewritten copy of the manuscript, prepared by Miss Toklas in 1933 and partly corrected by Miss Stein, which was given to the Yale University Library by Mr. Carl Van Vechten in November, 1940; it has been collated throughout with the original autograph manuscript which Miss Stein sent to the Library in July, 1946, only a few weeks before her death.

Donald Gallup

Sterling Memorial Library
Yale University

INTRODUCTION

MISS GERTRUDE STEIN, answering a question about her line
A rose is a rose is a rose is a rose,
once said with characteristic vehemence:

"Now listen! I'm no fool. I know that in daily life we don't say 'is a . . . is a . . . is a . . .'"

She knew that she was a difficult and an idiosyncratic author. She pursued her aims, however, with such conviction and intensity that occasionally she forgot that the results could be difficult to others. At such times the achievements she had made in writing, in "telling what she knew" (her most frequent formulization of the aim of writing) had to her the character of self-evident beauty and clarity. A friend, to whom she showed recently completed examples of her poetry, was frequently driven to reply sadly: "But you forget that I don't understand examples of your extremer styles." To this she would reply with a mixture of bewilderment, distress, and exasperation:

"But what's the difficulty? Just read the words on the paper. They're in English. Just read them. Be simple and you'll understand these things."

Now let me quote the whole speech from which the opening remark in this introduction has been extracted. A student in her seminar at the University of Chicago had asked her for an "explanation" of the famous line. She leaned forward giving all of herself to the questioner in that unforgettable way which has endeared her to hundreds of students and to hundreds of soldiers in two wars, trenchant, humorous, but above all urgently concerned over the enlightenment of even the most obtuse questioner:

"Now listen! Can't you see that when the language was new—as it was with Chaucer and Homer—the poet could use the name of a thing and the thing was really there? He could say 'O moon,' 'O sea,' 'O love' and the moon and the sea and love were really there. And can't you see that after hundreds of years had gone by and thousands of poems had been written, he could call on those words and find that they were

just wornout literary words? The excitingness of pure being had with-
drawn from them; they were just rather stale literary words. Now the
poet has to work in the excitingness of pure being; he has to get back
that intensity into the language. We all know that it's hard to write
poetry in a late age; and we know that you have to put some strangeness, something unexpected, into the structure of the sentence in order
to bring back vitality to the noun. Now it's not enough to be bizarre;
the strangeness in the sentence structure has to come from the poetic
gift, too. That's why it's doubly hard to be a poet in a late age. Now
you all have seen hundreds of poems about roses and you know in your
bones that the rose is not there. All those songs that sopranos sing as
encores about 'I have a garden; oh, what a garden!' Now I don't want
to put too much emphasis on that line, because it's just one line in a
longer poem. But I notice that you all know it; you make fun of it, but
you know it. Now listen! I'm no fool. I know that in daily life we don't
go around saying 'is a . . . is a . . . is a . . .' Yes, I'm no fool;
but I think that in that line the rose is red for the first time in English
poetry for a hundred years."

   This book is full of that "strangeness which must come from the
poetic gift" in order to restore intensity to images dusted over with
accustomedness and routine. It is not required in poetry alone; for Miss
Stein all intellectual activities—philosophical speculation, literary
criticism, narration—had to be refreshed at the source.
   There are certain of her idiosyncrasies which by this time should not
require discussion—for example, her punctuation and her recourse to
repetition. Readers who still baulk at these should not attempt to read
this volume, for it contains idiosyncrasies far more taxing to con-
ventional taste. The majority of readers ask of literature the kind of
pleasure they have always received; they want "more of the same";
they accept idiosyncrasy in author and period only when it has been
consecrated by a long-accumulated prestige, as in the cases of the
earliest and the latest of Shakespeare's styles, and in the poetry of
Donne, Gerard Manley Hopkins, or Emily Dickinson. They arrogate
to themselves a superiority in condemning the novels of Kafka or of the
later Joyce or the later Henry James, forgetting that they allow a no less
astonishing individuality to Laurence Sterne and to Rabelais.
   This work is for those who not only largely accord to others "an-

other's way," but who rejoice in the diversity of minds and the tension of difference.

Miss Stein once said:

"Every masterpiece came into the world with a measure of ugliness in it. That ugliness is the sign of the creator's struggle to say a new thing in a new way, for an artist can never repeat yesterday's success. And after every great creator there follows a second man who shows how it can be done easily. Picasso struggled and made his new thing and then Braque came along and showed how it could be done without pain. The Sistine Madonna of Raphael is all over the world, on grocers' calendars and on Christmas cards; everybody thinks it's an easy picture. It's our business as critics to stand in front of it and recover its ugliness."

This book is full of that kind of ugliness. It is perhaps not enough to say: "Be simple and you will understand these things"; but it is necessary to say: "Relax your predilection for the accustomed, the received, and be ready to accept an extreme example of idiosyncratic writing."

Distributed throughout Miss Stein's books and in the *Lectures in America* can be found an account of her successive discoveries and aims as a writer. She did not admit that the word "experiments" be applied to them. "Artists do not experiment. Experiment is what scientists do; they initiate an operation of unknown factors in order to be instructed by its results. An artist puts down what he knows and at every moment it is what he knows at that moment. If he is trying things out to see how they go he is a bad artist." A brief recapitulation of the history of her aims will help us to understand her work.

She left Radcliffe College, with William James's warm endorsement, to study psychology at Johns Hopkins University. There, as a research problem, her professor gave her a study of automatic writing. For this work she called upon her fellow students—the number ran into the hundreds—to serve as experimental subjects. Her interest, however, took an unexpected turn; she became more absorbed in the subjects' varying approach to the experiments than in the experiments themselves. They entered the room with alarm, with docility, with bravado, with gravity, with scorn, or with indifference. This striking variation reawoke within her an interest which had obsessed her even in very early childhood—the conviction that a description could be made of all the types of human character and that these types could be related to two basic types (she called them independent-dependents and dependent-independents). She left the university and settling in Paris, applied herself to the problem. The result was the novel of one thousand pages, *The Making of Americans,* which is at once an account of a large family from the time of the grandparents' coming to this country from Europe and a description of "everyone who is, or has been, or will be." She then went on to give in *A Long Gay Book* an account of all possible relations of two persons. This book, however, broke down soon after it began. Miss Stein had been invaded by another compelling problem: how, in our time, do you describe anything? In the previous centuries writers had managed pretty well by assembling a number of adjectives and adjectival clauses side by side; the reader "obeyed" by furnishing images and concepts in his mind and the resultant "thing" in the reader's mind corresponded fairly well with that in the writer's. Miss Stein felt that that process did not work any more. Her painter friends were showing clearly that the corresponding method of "description" had broken down in painting and she was sure that it had broken down in writing.

In the first place, words were no longer precise; they were full of extraneous matter. They were full of "remembering"—and describing a thing in front of us, an "objective thing," is no time for remembering. Even vision (a particularly overcharged word), even sight, had been dulled by remembering. The painters of the preceding generation, the Impressionists, had shown that. Hitherto people had known that, close to, a whitewashed wall had no purple in it; at a distance it may have a great deal of purple, but many painters had not allowed themselves to see purple in a distant whitewashed wall because they remembered that close to it was uniformly white. The Impressionists had shown us the red in green trees; the Postimpressionists showed us that out entire sense of form, our very view of things, was all distorted and distorting and "educated" and adjusted by memory. Miss Stein felt that writing must accomplish a revolution whereby it could report things as they were in themselves before our minds had appropriated them and robbed them of their objectivity "in pure existing." To this end she went about her house describing the objects she found there

in the series of short "poems" which make up the volume called
Tender Buttons.

Here is one of these:

Red Roses

A cool red rose and a pink cut pink, a collapse and a sold hole, a little
less hot.

Miss Stein had now entered upon a period of excited discovery, intense concentration, and enormous productivity. She went on to writing
portraits of her friends and of places. She revived an old interest in
drama and wrote scores of plays, many of which are themselves portraits of friends and of places. Two of her lectures in *Lectures in
America* describe her aims in these kinds of work. She meditated long
on the nature of narration and wrote the novel *Lucy Church Amiably.*
This novel is a description of a landscape near Bilignin, her summer
home in the south of France. Its subtitle and epigraph are: "A Novel
of Romantic Beauty and Nature and which Looks Like an Engrav-
ing . . . 'and with a nod she turned her head toward the falling
water. Amiably.' "

Those who had the opportunity of seeing Miss Stein in the daily
life of her home will never forget an impressive realization of her practice of meditating. She set aside a certain part of every day for it. In
Bilignin she would sit in her rocking chair facing the valley she has
described so often, holding one or the other of her dogs on her lap.
Following the practice of a lifetime she would rigorously pursue some
subject in thought, taking it up where she had left it on the previous
day. Her conversation would reveal the current preoccupation: it
would be the nature of "money," or "masterpieces," or "superstition,"
or "the Republican party." She had always been an omnivorous reader.
As a small girl she had sat for days at a time in a window seat in the
Marine Institute Library in San Francisco, an endowed institution with
few visitors, reading all Elizabethan literature, including its prose,
reading all Swift, Burke, and Defoe. Later in life her reading remained
as wide but was strangely nonselective. She read whatever books came
her way. ("I have a great deal of inertia. I need things from outside to
start me off.") The Church of England at Aix-les-Bains sold its Sunday School library, the accumulation of seventy years, at a few francs

for every ten volumes. They included some thirty minor English novels of the 'seventies, the stately lives of colonial governors, the lives of missionaries. She read them all. Any written thing had become sheer phenomenon; for the purposes of her reflections absence of quality was as instructive as quality. Quality was sufficiently supplied by Shakespeare whose works lay often at her hand. If there was any subject which drew her from her inertia and led her actually to seek out works it was American history and particularly books about the Civil War.

And always with her great relish for human beings she was listening to people. She was listening with genial absorption to the matters in which they were involved. "Everybody's life is full of stories; your life is full of stories; my life is full of stories. They are very occupying, but they are not really interesting. What is interesting is the way everyone tells their stories"; and at the same time she was listening to the tellers' revelation of their "basic nature." "If you listen, really listen, you will hear people repeating themselves. You will hear their pleading nature or their attacking nature or their asserting nature. People who say that I repeat too much do not really listen; they cannot hear that every moment of life is full of repeating. There is only one repeating that is really dead and that is when a thing is taught." She even listened intently to dog nature. The often-ridiculed statement is literally true that it was from listening to her French poodle Basket lapping water that she discovered the distinction between prose and poetry.

It can easily be understood that the questions she was asking concerning personality and the nature of language and concerning "how you tell a thing" would inevitably lead to the formulization of a metaphysics. In fact, I think it can be said that the fundamental occupation of Miss Stein's life was not the work of art but the shaping of a theory of knowledge, a theory of time, and a theory of the passions. These theories finally converged on the master-question: what are the various ways in which creativity works in everyone? That is the subject of this book. It is a subject which she was to develop more specifically in a book which of all her works is most closely related to this one: *The Geographical History of America or the Relation of Human Nature to the Human Mind*. It led also to a reconsideration of all literature, reflected in the beautiful lecture, "What are Masterpieces and Why are There So Few of Them?"

Miss Stein held a doctrine which permeates this book, which informs her theory of creativity, which plays a large part in her demonstration of what an American is, and which helps to explain some of the great difficulty which we feel in reading her work. It is the Doctrine of Audience; its literary aspect is considered in the Theory of the Moment of Recognition. In *The Geographical History of America* it is made to illustrate a Theory of Identity.

Let me enter into the subject by again quoting from her words in a conversation:

"Why is it that no preachers, no teachers, no orators, no parliamentary debaters ever have any ideas after the age of thirty-five? It is because when they talk they only hear what the audience is hearing. They get mixed up in their head and think that it is possible for one person to agree totally with another person; and when you think *that* you are lost and never have any ideas any more. Now what we know is formed in our head by thousands of small occasions in the daily life. By 'what we know' I do not mean, of course, what we learn from books, because that is of no importance at all. I mean what we really know, like our assurance about how we know anything, and what we know about the validity of the sentiments, and things like that. All the thousands of occasions in the daily life go into our head to form our ideas about these things. Now if we write, we write; and these things we know flow down our arm and come out on the page. The moment before we wrote them we did not really know we knew them; if they are in our head in the shape of words then that is all wrong and they will come out dead; but if we did not know we knew them until the moment of writing, then they come to us with a shock of surprise. That is the Moment of Recognition. Like God on the Seventh Day we look at it and say it is good. That is the moment that some people call inspiration, but I do not like the word inspiration, because it suggests that someone else is blowing that knowledge into you. It is not being blown into you; it is very much your own and was acquired by you in thousands of tiny occasions in your daily life. Now, of course, there is no audience at that moment. There is no one whom you are instructing, or fighting, or improving, or pleasing, or provoking. To others it may appear that you are doing all those things to them, but of course you are not. At that moment you are totally alone at this recognition of what you know. And of that thing which you have written you are the first and last audience. This thing which you have written is bought by other people and read by them. It goes through their eyes into their heads and they say they agree with it. But, of course, they cannot agree with it. The things they know have been built up by thousands of small occasions which are different from yours. They *say* they agree with you; what they mean is that they are aware that your pages have the vitality of a thing which sounds to them like someone else's knowing; it is consistent to its own world of what one person has really known. That is a great pleasure and the highest compliment they can pay it is to say that they agree with it.

"Now these preachers and orators may have had such moments of recognition when they were young; they may even have had them when they are addressing an audience—though that is very rare. After they have faced a great many audiences they begin to think that the audiences are literally understanding, literally agreeing with them, instead of merely being present at the vitality of these moments of recognition, at their surprising themselves with their own discovery of what they know. Then they gradually slip in more of the kind of ideas that people can agree with, ideas which are not really ideas at all, which are soothing but not exciting—oh, yes, they may be exciting as oratory, but they are not exciting as creation—and after a while they dry up and then they do not have any real ideas any more."

A portion of the ideas expressed above is found in the "Henry James" section of the present book:

Mr. Owen Young made a mistake, he said the only thing he wished his son to have was the power of clearly expressing his ideas. Not at all. It is not clarity that is desirable but force.

Clarity is of no importance because nobody listens and nobody knows what you mean, nor how clearly you mean what you mean. But if you have vitality enough of knowing enough of what you mean, somebody and sometime and sometimes a great many will have to realise that you know what you mean and so they will agree that you mean what you know, what you know you mean, which is as near as anybody can come to understanding any one.

Miss Stein never claimed that these doctrines were new. She delighted in finding them in the great works of the past. She was never tired of saying that all real knowledge is common knowledge; it lies sleeping within us; it is awakened in us when we hear it expressed by a person who is speaking or writing in a state of recognition.

From consciousness of audience, then, come all the evils of thinking, writing, and creating. In *The Geographical History of America* she illustrates the idea by distinguishing between our human nature and our human mind. Our human nature is a serpents' nest, all directed to audience; from it precede self-justification, jealousy, propaganda, individualism, moralizing, and edification. How comforting it is, and how ignobly pleased we are when we see it expressed in literature. The human mind, however, gazes at experience and without deflection by the insidious pressures from human nature tells what it sees and knows. Its subject matter is indeed human nature; to cite two of Miss Stein's favorites, *Hamlet* and *Pride and Prejudice* are about human nature, but not of it. The survival of masterpieces, and there are very few of them, is due to our astonishment that certain minds can occasionally report life without adulterating the report with the gratifying movements of their own self-assertion, their private quarrel with what it has been to be a human being.

Miss Stein pushed to its furthest extreme this position that at the moment of writing one rigorously excludes from the mind all thought of praise and blame, of persuasion or conciliation. In the early days she used to say: "I write for myself and strangers." Then she eliminated the strangers; then she had a great deal of trouble with the idea that one is an audience to oneself, which she solves in this book with the far-reaching concept: "I am not I when I see."

It has often seemed to me that Miss Stein was engaged in a series of spiritual exercises whose aim was to eliminate during the hours of writing all those whispers into the ear from the outside and inside world where audience dwells. She knew that she was the object of derision to many and to some extent the knowledge fortified her. Yet it is very moving to learn that on one occasion when a friend asked her what a writer most wanted, she replied, throwing up her hands and laughing, "Oh, praise, praise, praise!" Some of the devices that most exasperate readers—such as the capricious headings of subdivisions in her work, such sequences as Book IV, Book VII, Book VIII, Volume I—though in part they are there to make fun of pompous heads who pretend to an organic development and have no development, are at bottom merely attempts to nip in the bud by a drastic intrusion of apparent incoherence any ambition she may have felt within herself to woo for acceptance as a "respectable" philosopher. It should be noted that another philosopher who wrestled with the problem of restating the mind of man in the terms of our times and who has emerged as perhaps the most disturbing and stimulating voice of the nineteenth century—Sören Kierkegaard—delayed his recognition and "put off" his readers by many a mystification and by an occasional resort to almost Aristophanic buffoonery.

There is another evidence of Miss Stein's struggle to keep her audience out of her mind. *Four in America* is not a book which is the end and summary of her thoughts about the subjects she has chosen; it is the record of her thoughts, from the beginning, as she "closes in" on them. It is *being written* before our eyes; she does not, as other writers do, suppress and erase the hesitations, the recapitulations, the connectives, in order to give us the completed fine result of her meditations. She gives us the process. From time to time we hear her groping toward the next idea; we hear her cry of joy when she has found it; sometimes, it seems to me that we hear her reiterating the already achieved idea and, as it were, pumping it in order to force out the next development that lies hidden within it. We hear her talking to herself about the book that is growing and glowing (to borrow her often irritating habit of rhyming) within her. Many readers will not like this, but at least it is evidence that she is ensuring the purity of her indifference as to whether her readers will like it or not. It is as though she were afraid that if she went back and weeded out all these signs of groping and shaping and reassembling, if she gave us only the completed thoughts in their last best order, the truth would have slipped away like water through a sieve because such a final marshaling of her thoughts would have been directed toward audience. Her description of existence would be, like so many hundreds of thousands of descriptions of existence, like most literature—dead.

Another spiritual exercise she practices is no less disconcerting. She introduces what I like to call "the irruption of the daily life." If her two dogs are playing at her feet while she is writing she puts them into the text. She may suddenly introduce some phrases she has just heard over the garden wall. This resembles a practice that her friends the Post-impressionist painters occasionally resorted to. They pasted a subway ticket to the surface of their painting. The reality of a work of art is one reality; the reality of a "thing" is another reality; the juxtaposition of the two kinds of reality gives a bracing shock. It also insults the reader; but the reader is not present, nor even imagined. It refreshes in the writer the sense that the writer is all alone, alone with his thoughts and his struggle and even with his relation to the outside world that lies about him.

The fourth section of this book, by far the most difficult, seems to me to be full of these voices and irruptions. She is sitting on the terrace of her villa at Bilignin toward the end of day. The subject of George Washington comes toward her from a distance:

Autumn scenery is warm if the fog has lifted.
And the moon has set in the day-time in what may be drifting clouds. . . .
George Washington was and is the father of his country. . .
It should not be a disturbance if they can mistake a bird for a bat and a bat for a bird and find it friendly.

At first view the plan of this book appears to furnish little more than a witty diversion, a parlor game—what kind of novels would George Washington have written? what kind of military strategy would Henry James have devised? One soon discovers, however, that it is a very earnest game indeed. It asks about "how creativity works in any one," about the relations between personality and gifts, personality and genius. No less searchingly, it asks another question: what is an American and what makes him different from a citizen of any other country?

Soon after Miss Stein settled in France for an almost unbroken residence of over forty years a very unusual thing happened to her: she was really taken into a number of French homes. She was told their secrets, told their finances, and told their politics. That must seldom have happened to any American who was at once so loved, so tirelessly ready to listen to details, and who had so consuming a passion to reduce the multitudinous occasions of the daily life to psychological and philosophical laws.

In addition, she spent some time in England during the earlier part of the War of 1914–18. She spent a number of summers in Spain and related what she saw to the characters of her three close friends the Spanish painters, Picasso, Juan Gris, and Picabia. All the time, however, she was meeting and "listening" to Americans and the contacts with Europeans continued to sharpen her perception of specific American nature. When after thirty-five years' absence she returned to America and traveled it from coast to coast her delight was not only in the experience itself; it was also the delight of seeing her conclusions confirmed and extended.

The section on Ulysses S. Grant begins with a lively discussion of the relations between people and the Christian names they bear. She relates it to superstition and to religion, as later she will relate it to the spell cast by novelists, the novelist Henry James and the hypothetical novelist George Washington.

She is tracking down certain irrational ways we have of knowing things, of believing things, and of being governed by these ways of believing. Even the strongest minds have been nonplussed and rendered angry by the extent to which they can be caught up into belief by imaginative narration. One remembers St. Augustine's anguished repudiation of the hold which theatrical performances had taken of him in Carthage. "Novels are true," says Miss Stein. Similarly, great minds have tried to revolt from the sway that superstition can exert over them—involuntarily downcast by omens, predictions, recurrences of certain numbers—just as lesser minds can be given courage by a palm reading and can be crossed with fear by a broken mirror. There is no "truth" in these things, people say; but perhaps man knows nothing and will never know anything; the important thing is that he behaves as though he knew something and the irrational ways of knowing which are found in religion and superstition and in submission to a novel are among the more powerful driving forces toward how he behaves.

Miss Stein is talking about religion throughout this section and she is furnishing analogies to the kind of "knowing" that goes to make up religious belief. One of them is the haunting sense that your name is the right name for you.

Religion, as Miss Stein uses the term, has very little to do with cults and dogma, particularly in America. She makes a score of attempts to define it, but the attempts result in fragmentary analogies, straining the syntax of the English language to express flashes of insight. Religion is what a person knows—knows beyond knowing, knows beyond anyone's power to teach him—about his relation to the existence in which he finds himself. It is the tacit assumption that governs his "doing anything that he does do," his creativity. "Religion is what is alright if they have to have their ups and downs." "Religion is not a surprise but it is exciting." "There is no advice in American religion." "American religion is what they could not compare with themselves." "Nobody in America need be careful to be alone, not in American religion . . ."

To illustrate what American religion is she first chooses the figure of a camp meeting. There is no leader, or to put it more exactly, there is a leader but the people are not led. Here is the first striking difference from European religion. It is in the open; there is even some deliberation as to whether the trees have to be there. Just as we hear that Americans have no home, just because their whole country is their home, so their church really has no house. The fact is Americans do not localize anything, not even themselves, as the whole book constantly reiterates. Here again we are a long way from European religion. Moreover, American religion is thanking, not supplication. Americans do not even wish. We shall see the extent to which they do not "wait"; they are not "ready," except in limited contingencies, they do not "prepare"—so little does an American believe that one forces circumstances to one's will. It is at the very heart of American religion that the majority of Americans "like what they have," and readers of *The Geographical History of America* will see how this relative absence of resenting the universe, despising the universe, trying to subjugate or reshape a "destiny" derives from the physical constitution of our country and the problems our pioneers met. Now in a camp meeting some walk up and down, some stand, some sing, some kneel, some wail; there is a leader but they are not led; and a congregation of four hundred is not four hundred, but it is one and one and one and one . . . up to four hundred.

The foregoing does not mean that Americans are passive. The true passivity, that is the true slavery and the true ineffectiveness, is to wish and to wait and to yearn and to conspire. Nor does the group that is one and one and one, and so on, mean that the American is an uncurbed individualist, for "they all go forward together." "They act as if they all go together one by one and so any one is not leading." "Go forward" has no moralizing sense; in Gertrude Stein it is hard to find a moralizing sense. Moralizing comes from that realm of belief which is acquired, learned, arrogated to oneself and promulgated; but which is not truly believed or lived by.

The passage to the effect that Americans cannot earn a living or be a success is likely to cause the bewildered astonishment that it first aroused in Miss Stein. ("Now, Lizzie, do you understand?") It is conceded that some Americans can make money, and that they can do what they have to do and that they can become "names which everyone knows," but that is not the same thing. Again Miss Stein is seeing Americans against her immense knowledge of French domestic life, compared to which the American relation to money is frivolous and the American relation to the whole practical side of life is without perseverance, foresight, or thorough application. The French would put it overwhelmingly that we are not *"serieux."* In conversation, Miss Stein went even further; she said that "Americans are really only happy when they are failures," and laughing deeply she would furnish a wealth of illustration. Again the reader should be warned against interpreting this passage in moralizing terms; this is not the sentimental commonplace that life's failures are the true successes nor does it mean that Americans are unworldly knight errants. An American's inability to make a living is not a consequence of his "values" but of the way his mind works in him.

The portrait of an American is then beginning to assemble about the image of General Grant and his hypothetical alter ego, Hiram Grant, retired from the army and become very busily a failure in the harness store at Galena, Illinois. He did not wait for the great position that would someday fall to him, because Americans do not wait, that is they do not live in the expectation that circumstance is coming toward them bearing gifts. There is no animism in American religion. The skies do not pity nor punish nor bring gifts. Nor does her American yearn, strain, or intrigue for the situations he may profit by; he is what he is, and what he *is,* not what he *wills,* is his expression. Some of the most exasperating of Miss Stein's phrases are employed to express this aspect of her subject. She seems to have a low opinion of the verb "sit" which to her expresses both the passivity and the expectancy which are not present in her American. Apparently, the word "there" and the verbs "come" and "go" all imply a degree of intention that is not in her Americans. So we get such upsetting combinations of these usages as: "Ulysses Simpson Grant was there as often as he came but he never came."

All this prepares us for the statement that Americans never die; they are killed or they go away, but they are not dead. This is in great contrast, of course, to the Europeans who "wait for" their death, prepare, resist, foresee, bewail, or accept their death. This she puts down to

the American sky, which is not really a sky but is just air; but it is
obviously related to the other elements of the American religion, that
all you have is in every moment of your consciousness (and that you
like all that you have) and so self-contained is every moment of consciousness that there is nothing left over for expectation or memory.
The American, then, who has lost that moment of consciousness is not
that European thing called "dead"—so fraught with immemorial con-
notations—he has gone away. For this Miss Stein finds the striking
image that every American is an only child—is *one,* has everything,
and is the center of everything—is then naturally very solemn and
cannot die.

This is followed by an apparently difficult passage which, however,
yields us some light on a number of Miss Stein's most characteristic
locutions. General Grant was not "one of two" or "one of three"; for
relief or guidance or comfort or support he did not ally himself with
anyone else and even when he came to fill that high station for which
he had not been waiting he was "not differently surrounded by himself"—surrounded, of course, he was, as we all are, but "surround does
not mean surrender" (and surrender is here not the act of war but the
loss of one's own knowing: "This is what I mean and this will I do").

So we begin to see what kind of a saint General Grant would have
been if he had been a leader in religion. And now we see another reason
why I went to some length to discuss Miss Stein's theory of Audience
and her theory of the distinction between human nature and the
human mind. It looks as though General Ulysses S. Grant and the saint
he might have been had it in common that they did not listen to those
seductive appeals from the Audience which keep crowding up from
human nature. Neither Grant waited nor was anxious; neither came
nor sat; both "knew what they knew at the moment of knowing it," a
knowledge unsullied by expectation or memory. They did not let will
or determination order them about; they did what they did, but they
did not set about to do what they were to do.

One word hovers over the entire book and is never spoken. It is the
word "abstract." American religion is presented as very abstract, and
so are the mentalities of the Americans described here who are certainly
prototypes of the generalized American. In *The Geographical History
of America* she goes on to explain that such minds are so formed by
the physical character of the environment in which they live. "Every-

one is as their land and water and sky are," and in America there is no
sky—there is just air; there is just "up"; the majority of Americans, in
addition, either know the straight line of the sea or the lake, or they
know a land so devoid of natural features that "when they made the
boundary of a State they have to make it with a straight line." In
European geography there are no boundaries which are straight lines.

The section on Wilbur Wright begins with another teasing play with
Christian names. The reader can now share Miss Stein's delighted con-
sternation on receiving a letter from a man named Ulysses Lee. "And
there is nothing more to be said is there. Names call to names as birds
call to birds." We have learned what a "Ulysses" nature is; a nature
of that degree of abstraction could conceivably be born into a situation
in which he would find himself called Ulysses Lee.

In driving through Le Mans Miss Stein once came upon the monument which the French had raised to Wilbur Wright. She tells us that
she was struck with the "funny feeling" that Wilbur Wright was not
there. France contains many monuments to its eminent dead and in a
way she felt that their eminent dead were there. As she has told us,
Americans do not die, they go away; but it was very clear that they do
not go away to their monuments. This set her brooding again about
American religion and American death and about Wilbur Wright and
how he made what he made. Presently she found a relationship between
aviation and painting and between painting and acting.

Now a writer is not confronted by his past books. They are not
even there in his mind, staring at him. His past work is not an audience
to him. He is not his work and he is not connected to his work, save
at the moment of creation. All painters, however, and particularly
European painters, are surrounded by their paintings, even if their
paintings are distributed all over the world. They are "extended" to
their paintings. They are not alone. And the paintings are not "left"—
are not relegated to a place outside consciousness. We are repeatedly
told that no painting can be "left."

This has something to do with seeing, and leads to a similar situation
in actors and in Wilbur Wright. Actors in a profound sense see rather
than hear what they say. (The words are but a small part of the creativity in their art and the words having been created in the "recognition"
of the dramatist are resumed by the actor into his total creation which is

preponderantly visual. He "paints" a role employing the words of the dramatist as the raw material of his painting, just as his face, body, voice, and dress are raw material. It is in this sense that he "sees what he says.")

These creators who see their past work are eternally surrounded by it and are not alone. This is not urged as a reproach upon them; it is the character of their creativity; nor is their past work an audience to them in a bad sense, for they are their creativity, past and present. In the vocabulary of Miss Stein seeing always stands high. She enjoyed repeating that "seeing is believing." Readers will remark that among these thousands of references to creativity there is no reference to music. "Music is for adolescents" she used to say. The eye is closer to the human mind, the ear to human nature. She had passed through a phase of her life as an impassioned and informed music-lover and had put it behind her. Only once have I heard her concede that music—it was after a hearing of Beethoven's "Archduke" Trio—can occasionally issue from the human mind.

A reader having reached the middle point in the Wilbur Wright section is presumably becoming accustomed to Miss Stein's disregard for the first or generally received meanings of words and to her powerful compressions. (They have a relationship by contrast with her repetitions: a repetition is a small degree of progression by alteration and emphasis; a compression is a sweeping summary or a violent leap into new matter.) A reader is ready for such a passage as the following (the punctuation is impertinently mine): "A painting is something seen after it has been done and—in this way—left alone; nobody can say: 'he—or I—left it alone.' No painting is left alone."

The airplane was that kind of creation and the man whose work it was to make the flying machine and to fly it saw himself moving; he was in his creation as a painter is in and of his painting.

There are many difficulties in this section for which I am not competent to furnish a gloss. The day will come when devoted readers of Miss Stein will furnish a lexicon of her locutions. There are hundreds of them which may strike a first reader as incoherent expressions thrown off at random; but they are found recurringly distributed throughout her work. The task of her future commentators will consist in tracing them to their earliest appearances embedded in a context which furnishes the meaning they held for her. Thereafter they became bricks in her building, implements in her meditation. To her their meaning is "self-evident"; she forgets that we have not participated in the systematic meditation which was her life.

I leave to the reader's contemplation also the spectacle of the extraordinary emotion which accumulates toward the end of each of these sections. Miss Stein loves, overwhelmingly loves, each of the heroes of this volume. "Who knows what Grant did. I do." "It is Ulysses S. Grant that is interesting, very interesting." "I cannot think of Ulysses Simpson Grant without tears." "Wilbur Wright is fine." "East and West. George Washington is best."

The Henry James section begins with Miss Stein's account of how she came to make an important discovery concerning writing. It is a curious thing to me that in each of her retellings of this story she has omitted a fact that throws further light on it. This fact is that when she wrote the poems called *Before the Flowers of Friendship Faded Friendship Faded* she began writing them as translations of a group of poems in French by her friend Georges Hugnet. They are far from being literal translations, even in the beginning, but they take their point of departure from his poems, and they remained, as her discussion shows, "the poems he would have written if he had written them."

Hence, she was not writing "what she wrote, but what she intended to write." A sort of ventriloquism had introduced itself into the process of writing, and she became aware that the words had a sort of smoothness which they did not have in the poems which she wrote "from herself alone." Suddenly this smoothness reminded her of a smoothness she had long noticed in Shakespeare's Sonnets. She says (in the fourth lecture on *Narration*):

I concluded then that Shakespeare's sonnets were not written to express his own emotion. I concluded he put down what some one told him to do as their feeling which they definitely had for each sonnet as their feeling and that is the reason that the words in the sonnets come out with a smooth feeling with no vibration in them such as the words in all his plays have as they come out from them.

Many scholars have reached a similar conclusion as to Shakespeare's Sonnets, and not only in regard to the series written on the preposterous theme "Go, young man, and get married in order that you may leave a copy of your excellences to the afterworld."

Miss Stein was perhaps a little nettled to find also that the poems of *Before the Flowers of Friendship Faded* gave more pleasure to her friends than her earlier poems had given. This discovery led her straight to the problem of audience. There are two kinds of writing: the kind in which the words mean what they say and the kind in which the *"meaning has to be meant as something [that] has been learned"*—it has been written to satisfy a preconceived notion as to what it will be like when it is finished, or to satisfy someone else's expectation of it. It is surprising that at this stage of drawing up this distinction she expresses so little disapproval of the second type of writing. She appears to be reconciled to it, it is the way in which the majority of all books have been written.

Henry James, it appears, wrote in a combination of the two ways of writing. In this he resembled a general whose activity consists in doing what he has to do in a situation that has already been prepared. In a general's work for a while *"nothing happens together and then all of a sudden it all happens together."* For a general and for Henry James *"everything that could happen or not happen would have had a preparation."*

This treatment of Henry James does indeed awaken a feeling which one had had about his work. It does not mean that other novelists like Fielding, Jane Austen, and Anthony Trollope—to name three for whom she had the highest admiration—did not likewise follow a design and know well in advance the pattern their book was to take. Henry James went further; he finished the book before he wrote it; he wrote the book to resemble a book which he had completely envisaged. Like a general he arrived on a scene which had already been prepared or as we are repeatedly told had "been begun." He was to an unprecedented degree an audience to his own composition. We could wish that Miss Stein had helped us through these subtle distinctions by an occasional specific illustration. One is indebted to her, however, for two exquisite characterizations of Henry James's quality. She is speaking of a woman who lived in a chateau near Belley: *"She lived alone and in the country and so did Henry James. She was heavy set and seductive and so was Henry James. She was slow in movement and light in speech and could change her speech without changing her words so that at one time her speech was delicate and witty and at another time slow and troubling and so was that of Henry James."* And again: *"He had no fortune and misfortune and nevertheless he had no distress and no relief from any*

*pang . . . He had no failure and no success and he had no relief from
any failure and he had no relief from any distress."*

There is an extended portion of this section in which Miss Stein
gradually changes into a different style. It is the style of the "Portraits."
In fact, when she alludes to this book in one of her *Narration* lectures,
she calls it a book of portraits. In her lecture "Portraits and Repetition"
she says:

*"And so I am trying to tell you what doing portraits meant to me,
I had to find out what it was inside any one, and by any one I mean
every one. I had to find out inside every one what was in them that
was intrinsically exciting and I had to find out not by what they said
not by what they did not by how much or how little they resembled any
other one but I had to find out by the intensity of movement that there
was inside in any one of them."*

In another place in the lecture she calls this work catching *"the
rhythm of personality."* Opinions on this extreme style vary even
among Miss Stein's greatest admirers. Some assure us that from the first
reading they obtain a clear image of the personality so described; others
acknowledge occasional flashes of insight but hold that Miss Stein was
mistaken in thinking that she had been able to convey the "movement"
of her sitters' personalities to anyone but herself. Readers who are
indebted to her other writings for so wide a variety of pleasures—for
the narrative brilliance of *The Autobiography of Alice B. Toklas,* the
massive grasp of *The Making of Americans,* the critical insight and
aphoristic skill of her lectures, the illumination and the trenchant thinking about fundamentals contained in the present book—such readers
will return again and again to the most difficult pages not willingly
conceding that these are forever closed to them.

The fourth section, "Scenery and George Washington," has the subtitle "A Novel or a Play." Its characters are "Scenery" and "George
Washington." The section opens, as I have said, with an evocation of
the valley below her villa at Bilignin toward which comes, as from a
distance, the figure of Washington and the inquiry as to what kind of
novels he would have written.

Now Miss Stein felt that the novel was threatened with extinction
and she was much concerned with whether it could be saved. Her fears
concerning it were not based, as those of many critics have been, on the

fact that the assumption of omniscience on the part of the storyteller is untenable in our time. Her objection was that what happens "from outside" is no longer important to us, that we are aware of so much happening that the event is no longer exciting; and that we no longer feel that the sequence of events, the succession in time, is of much significance. As she says in the fourth *Narration* lecture:

"... *and this has come to be a natural thing in a perfectly natural way that the narrative of today is not a narrative of succession as all the writing for a good many hundreds of years has been.* ... *There is at present not a sense of anything being successively happening, moving is in every direction beginning and ending is not really exciting, anything is anything, anything is happening* ..."

And in the lecture "Portraits and Repetition" she says:

"*A thing you all know is that in the three novels written in this generation that are the important things written in this generation, there is, in none of them a story. There is none in Proust in The Making of Americans or in Ulysses.*"

Miss Stein interrupts her discussion to give samples of the event-novel, the succession-novel, and she assures us that is not the kind of novel George Washington wrote. What he wrote was "the great American novel," an entirely new kind of novel and a thing which, if we can know it, will throw invaluable light on the American nature. With what she calls "Volume VI" begins a flood of definitions, that is analogical definitions of what this novel is, just as the Grant section furnished a flood of descriptions of what "American religion" is.

In the first place, it has to do with the American time-sense. In the lecture "What is English Literature" she shows how the English, living for centuries their *"daily island life,"* made their literature out of it. *"They relied on it so completely that they did not describe it they just had it and told it* ... *In America* ... *the daily everything was not the daily living and generally speaking there is not a daily everything. They do not live every day* ... *and so they do not have this as something they are telling."* We are back at the abstractedness of the American mind. It does not draw its assurance of knowing anything from an intense localization in time and place. The endless procession of phenomena separate themselves from their specific contingency and reform themselves as a generalized knowing.

"*And so* ... *Henry James just went on doing what American*

literature had always done, the form was always the form of the con-
temporary English one, but the disembodied way of disconnecting
something from anything and anything from something was the
American one . . . Some say that it is repression, but no it is not
repression it is a lack of connection, of there being no connection with
living and daily living because there is none, that makes American
writing what it always has been and what it will continue to become."

It should be unnecessary to say that this George Washington was not
a novelist because he aesthetically composed his life or because he stood
off at a distance and viewed his life. A novelist is sovereign over the
elements of his imagined world; but they have also an objective life
(derived from the "knowing" that he has acquired); he may not force
or wrench them, nor make them report a fairer world than he has
experienced. We seem to be told by Miss Stein that George Washington moved among events like a novelist among his characters at the
moment of their creation. ("*I am fond of talking about Napoleon but*
that has nothing to do with novel writing. Napoleon could not write
a novel, not he. Washington could. And did.") And because he was
an American novelist, George Washington was disattached from the
concrete and the specific. He could and did love concrete things. ("*He*
was charmed with the dresses of the little baby"—how astonishing are
Miss Stein's ways of enclosing the general in the specific! That is an
example of the writing which she exalts in the Henry James section,
where the "*writing and the writer are alike,*" of a "*sound heard by the*
eyes," and that "*does not mean what it says because it just is*"—that is,
lands squarely on its truth and is only watered down by "preparation"
and explanation, as I have watered it down here.) George Washington's love of the concrete in our human life and his pleasure in baby-
dresses was of the American order; it tended to transmute its experiences
from things of human nature to things of the human mind. The human
mind cannot be consoled by things nor rendered proud; it does not
preach nor despise; it merely sees and tells what it sees. Such a novel
George Washington was writing every day.

The pages begin to bristle with Miss Stein's most idiosyncratic expressions and we are again in the "portrait" style. This introduction is
already too long to permit of an attempt to wrestle with them. The
solution of many of them, however, can be found elsewhere in Miss
Stein's work. For example, the long passage on Washington's youth

beginning with the disconcerting phrases: *"He could just smile if he was born already . . . And he was not born. Oh indeed no he was not born,"* has a history in her work. As early as *A Long Gay Book* Miss Stein was observing that many people are rendered uneasy, are even crippled, by the thought that they were once helpless babies, passed about and tended by others. The dignity of their human mind (which, of course, knows no age) is undermined by thoughts of themselves in infancy. It is this idea which grows into fuller statement in *The Geographical History of America* in the development of the astonishing question: *"What is the use of being a little boy if you are going to grow up to be a man?"*

The word "tears" occurs frequently in this book. What things in our human lot seem to have moved Miss Stein to tears? It was not the misfortunes of our human nature, though she was a greatly sympathetic resource to her friends when their griefs were real. What moved her deeply was the struggle of the human mind in its work which is to know. It was of Henry James's mind (and the phrase applies as beautifully to those great heroines of his last novels who live not to assert themselves but to understand) that she says *"he had no relief from any pang."*

She said to me once: "Everyone when they are young has a little bit of genius, that is they really do listen. They can listen and talk at the same time. Then they grow a little older and many of them get tired and they listen less and less. But some, a very few continue to listen. And finally they get very old and they do not listen any more. That is very sad; let us not talk about that." This book is by an impassioned listener to life. Even up to her last years she listened to all comers, to "how their knowing came out of them." Hundreds of our soldiers, scoffing and incredulous but urged on by their companions, came up to Paris "to see the Eiffel Tower and Gertrude Stein." They called and found bent upon them those gay and challenging eyes and that attention that asked nothing less of them than their genius. Neither her company nor her books were for those who have grown tired of listening. It was an irony that she did her work in a world in which for many reasons and for many appalling reasons people have so tired.

Hamden, Connecticut   Thornton Wilder
July, 1947

What They Thought and Bought

FOUR IN AMERICA

If Ulysses S. Grant had been a religious leader who was to become a saint what would he have done.

If the Wright brothers had been artists that is painters what would they have done.

If Henry James had been a general what would he have had to do.

If General Washington had been a writer that is a novelist what would he do.

GRANT

GRANT in his very early life was under obligation to an older man and took his name.

If he had remained Hiram Ulysses, as he was born, would he have been ultimately successful. I am unable to doubt it. But would it have been possible for him to have been called United States Grant or Unconditional Surrender Grant. It would not Naturally it would not.

If he had remained Hiram Ulysses Grant would it, in the meantime, have had something to do with what he would do if he were a religious leader or a saint. I mean by this, if he had been Hiram Ulysses Grant would he have been a religious leader or a saint, would he have had to be. I cannot doubt it.

I have never known any one named Ulysses. Nor Hiram. And so, names, by the way, names have a way of being attached to those that bear them.

Does the Christian name mean more than the surname. Yes I think so.

Surnames are family names and so in the history of the individual it is of no importance what the family name is or has been. This is not what everybody says but everybody knows that it is what I say and I say what they, that is everybody knows.

Really and truly the surname makes no difference, it is the first or Christian name that counts, that is what makes one be as they are. Of course you all know this.

I have found it to be a fact, that little as one can think it, which is the same as say they do not believe it, it is nevertheless true that the names that are given, the given name or the Christian name does or do denote character and career.

And now why is this so.

One might think it would be so if for instance as is done in some countries a given name or first name or Christian name is given on the day a saint was born, it might be that if they were all born around the same day and so had the same name and the saint already had that name that they would all have the same character having been born on the same day. It might be so. But is it so. This I say I do not know but I do know. No it is not so.

When you are born as well as where and how perhaps does make a difference and perhaps not. It does make a difference that everybody born at any time under any condition is named a name, they have the career and the character of that name.

And now I will tell you why I have said so.

They might say, but some names are made up. And then there is only one, only one with such a name. When names are made up, well then names are made up. That again may be something else. This I know nothing about not having met enough to know how they do it.

How many names are there. A good many. But after all, most of us know, not so very many. And these we know very well.

Think, everybody think.

We often do know a great many having the same name, know them around the same time and before and after not any or before and after not many.

Name any name and then remember everybody you ever knew who bore that name. Are they all alike. I think so.

You will come to believe me when I say things like that.

I have only known one named Elmer but there are others, some in novels and some in books.

If I could be sure I would say that they were all alike. They have it in common, that they are known when they come in, that they have followers even when they sit still, that some one else gives them largely of something and that sooner or later they will rest, they will rest fairly soon, they do just rest. No one need know that they have not only not rested before. Oh follow me while I wait. This is what they all say, the Elmers every day and fairly early, they prefer moderately early to very late.

Now let us leave Elmer.

I have known a quantity of Georges, a quantity of Georges. Are they alike. Yes I think so. I may even say I know so. Have they the same character and career. Certainly, certainly. Is it sometimes louder and sometimes softer and sometimes stronger and sometimes weaker and yet always it looks alike. Certainly it does. I think if you will all think about all the Georges you have ever known you will see how right I am.

Take the name of Virgil, I have known one Virgil, but I have also seen others. I am sure that they are alike, not only that they are, but as has been said of one of them, they have a great deal of satisfaction. It is not true of them indeed that they can be satisfied but that indeed they have a great deal of satisfaction. I wonder whether the original Virgil was like that. Anybody can tell me that he was. This I do not need to know.

I have known a great many Pauls. Of one of them I have even tried to change the name, unsuccessfully. I know just what Pauls are like even though they differ. What are they like. They are alike that insofar as it is possible, nobody, that is not any woman ever really loves any one of them. Now just think of that and think how true it is. None of them not one of them have been really loved by any woman. They have been married and sometimes not married, and anything can be true of them, but they have never, dear me never, been ever loved by any woman. That is what no Paul can say.

Paul can be joined to Peter, that makes it different, Paul can be joined to other names which go together. That makes it a little different although half of it is just the same.

I have known Peters but more in French as Pierres. Let us not stop to listen about them or to them, at least not now.

I have known Francises three Francises, they were alike, nobody can deny, that the three Francises I knew are alike. They are like each other and like the kings that were called Francis and the saint, the saint seems different but was he. No indeed he was not.

The Francises are very beautiful to hear to see and to do. In every way. They are so beautifully heard, seen and done. They are not only beautiful in themselves but as it. And beside they are simple. They love birds, or dogs, they are joined to this and one. Can you feel a Francis now. I do. And they succeed too. To be always through and through beside being one and won. No Francis is ever two.

I have known Marguerites, I still know them. I know something about them, but really they or this cannot be interesting. Do you remember how she was in the opera. Well that is the way they are. They always make that mistake and nobody can blame them, nor do they. Of course they do not. As they are married or single women, with no one to do anything about them. Beside which, they are not better than they can do, although they will continue to do that thing. You can depend upon them. I did.

I have known Helens and Jennies, one of each of them but I know that the name is Jenny or Helen and that that is alright.

I have known a few Henrys, very few. There have been good descriptions of Henrys. Later on I will mention a few of them.

I have known two Michaels, I can separate them. And I do. Although both of them, like the only other one, is able to do anything which makes them relished and loved, like they should be loved.

I have known two Sarahs, they are somewhat alike, but really I like what I like. I like Sarahs. They do and they do not come into history.

Alices I do not mention although I have always known what I thought about Alices. And what do I think about Alices, or more than that, they are always little if they are not big but that is always enough let well enough alone.

I wish you to see that this which is a digression leads me up to first names and the characters that go with them. The characters that go with them have been suggested to me by my experience with those who bear them.

There are names I avoid mentioning and others that I forget when I do not think of them. But wait. Anybody can add something and some can add everything. Is not this a thing to say. Of course it is.

Hiram Ulysses Grant's name was changed to Ulysses Simpson Grant. He was born. After he was born his name was changed. This really does not and should not make any difference. Because after all he had been born and he had been named. But did it make a difference. Yes I think so. Because after all what was his name. And since, as we now know, it does make a difference, of course it did make a difference.

I often think about a great many who have been born and have been named. As all of them are.

It does make all the difference that they are named and the Christian or first name is more important than the last or surname. I say last because some people have more than one first or Christian name, or more than one last or surname; and this is sometimes important.

Hiram Ulysses Grant, Ulysses Simpson Grant, and so forth.

I try to think that I like the name of Hiram or even of Ulysses but really I do not. Why do I not. Because I never had the habit of saying either one or the other as the name of some one, while I have had the habit of saying Grant, and Grant is a name.

I have never as a matter of fact, no one has, as a matter of fact, ever called any one Ulysses or Hiram, at least where I heard them calling.

Can you see why this brings us again to religion. It does, names and religion. Names and religion are always connected just like that. Nobody interferes between names and religion.

Religion. They like religion.

Why do they like religion.

They like religion because if they like religion, they like what they will be, as having religion. They like religion, they like names, they like names and religion; they like it just like that.

So, for the moment forgetting religion that is to say not forgetting but for the moment not remembering religion, we say, Grant. What was Grant.

Grant was first an army officer, then not an army officer. Then he was a general and then a lieutenant general. This was a rank which was made for him especially. It meant that he was alone in this way.

When the war, his war, was over, he let the soldiers, the other soldiers as well as his soldiers take their horses and their guns with them so that they could plough the ground and shoot rabbits.

Once upon a time I told this story to a frenchman, he was very moved by it and said, no one in France had ever heard of it.

What would Grant have been if he had been important in religion, instead of having been important in being what he had been.

In the beginning if he had been going to be important in religion, what would he have been then, before he came to be important as he was, and while he was still earning a living. If he had been going to be important in religion would he have been then when he was earning his living, would he have been so busy doing nothing.

He did not really earn a living, because, like so many men, that is people, it is hard to earn a living.

If no one earned a living, some people can, but most people do not, that is to say, if they live, they live. Most people live.

Everybody knows that in a kind of way it is hard if not almost impossible to earn their living. Grant did this and knew this. He could, if he had done this, that is not earned a living, and knew this, that he did not earn a living, he would have been important in religion, he would have been, but of course he would have been, a leader in religion, he might have been a saint in a religion.

Everybody knows everybody knew, that Grant did not earn a living, and as it went on, it did not make of him a leader in religion, it left him so that no one was to blame. And then there he was, just as if everybody knew his name.

Does being important make being important have any meaning. Yes it does.

What would have been the effect if Grant had waited longer to be important in religion than he had waited to be important in war.

In either case he would not have earned a living before he was important either in religion or in war. That is the one thing they have in common religion and war this which nobody can deny.

In any case would he have earned a living. No. Not, as in any case so many in any case cannot, do not earn a living.

In either case he was not waiting. Why. Because, he would not have waited. Waited means, that he knew, if he could know, that it was coming.

Grant was not like that, he was not earning a living. Of course he did not know what there had been. If he had known what there had been, he would not then even then have been waiting.

Waiting means something if something is coming.

Grant was never waiting. No of course not. He was not earning a living, so of course not, there was no waiting in his living.

Supposing he was to be a great religious leader, would he have been waiting. Not at all. There is no blame for him, in his not being one waiting.

May I ask does or did Grant, Ulysses S. Grant mean, that he never is or was to wait. No he never does or did, mean to wait. No neither he or any one is ever waiting, not if they are like or alike with him.

Waiting means that they could know what was coming for him or before him, in other words that he could earn a living.

It might be that he would have been, not could have been but would have been, a great religious leader, but neither he nor any one is ever waiting.

He would not, not have been waiting but there is really no such thing as waiting for him or for any one who was not earning a living. Just think of that word wait. Not, we wait. See how it means, earn a living.

Think everybody think again. What is religion.

How could Grant have been a great religious leader. This is easy to see.

Religion in one way is why they look as if they heard. But he has nothing to do with heard or wait, he, Grant.

He does not look as if he heard, he does not even look as if he saw. Not in his photograph.

He had a beard in his photograph. This does not make or mar a religion. What is religion.

Now we have two things wait and heard. Neither can be there if Grant did not make a living, and he certainly did not. If not. Why not. Everybody knows that there is no if, anybody knows that he did not. He did not make a living.

Religion is what they hear when they hear, and they all hear. What do they hear.

Grant was not there to hear but this was alright, alright for him. Grant was there, which is the same as there hearing, he was here.

How well I remember which one I meant when I first heard of Ulysses Simpson Grant, when I first heard of Hiram Ulysses Grant. That is the only way to hear, you hear that he was there. Of course nobody misplaces that.

What does and what can Grant mean. Ulysses Simpson Grant. Slowly one finds oneself attaching oneself to Hiram Ulysses and so everything changes. He is a leader in religion. Understand that but do not hear this or wait for that. No not they. Hiram Ulysses Grant. And so as well as if it did, everything changes.

America is always building a nation, even now, when anybody might think a nation had been built.

And if a nation has been built there is only a people.

But when they are always building a nation then there is not only, only a people, there is no waiting.

Nobody can reconcile waiting with a pioneer. And they, they are always here, just dear me, a pioneer.

When they left home, when anybody left home, when they all left home, and in America and at that time, and as now, they all left home, when they left home, they went away from home, from any home, from their home, and they left home, never to see home again.

All is theirs, a whole country is their home, only they left their home. Yes they did, then and now, they left their home then and now. They can stay anywhere.

What is religion. Religion is, if it is, a camp-meeting.

Why is or are Americans different from others. Because they have no home to which to go, and so, why wait to come and go, why hear, why not, or hear. Why earn a living to say so. All this is so but not names. Nobody hears names, names are. Christian names or first names. But I have gone into that.

Religion and names. Yes that is so.

A camp-meeting can be a meeting in the woods or anywhere, just as they say it is. No one knows whose country is whose, as they are all there, and never heard of any other really.

That is why there is no us to hear or hear. Did they, any of them, ever hear either of any other country or any other camp-meeting.

Camp-meeting. Tenting to-night, tenting to-night, tenting on the old camp-ground. Which is which. All of which is, my country 'tis of thee, a camp-meeting.

What was Hiram Ulysses Grant before he changed.

Grant saw no one when he came and when he came he was not sitting, no not Grant. Of course he could sit, but it was not the custom.

I should think so, I could think that I saw them which may be why they were there. They can stand still in place of where. They can sit, but not there. Oh dear me, not where.

Do you see what I mean. Let me explain and make it plain.

Now that sounds like this, they can stand still in place of where. But do you see, that is just the way they did sit or stand or do yet do.

For instance did it make any difference that they were soldiers too or just before or just after or not at all. Of course, not at all, about standing.

Think everybody think, and you will see them too. Of course you do. Anybody can too. Which of course yes they do. And did. Stand and sit. Sit and stand. Just stand. And.

Grant was not ready, neither to stay nor to go away, nor to wait, and so Hiram Grant was a leader in religion. Anybody can cry that Ulysses Simpson Grant was not so. He was not aware of it. No one could bother him with this. If he had not been.

When is there religion.

There always is religion.

There always would have been Hiram. There can be no decade nor played without Ulysses Simpson. Do not these names begin to mean something to you. If not why not.

Hiram Ulysses Grant was a leader in religion. That came to him not as an easy thing but as a thing for which he was not waiting. He was not waiting for anything. Do I not tell you there is not any such thing as waiting, not for any one, not because any one, and because chiefly every one cannot earn a living.

Hiram Ulysses Grant was a leader in religion. Every little while he, not waiting, and at any rate no one could dispute anything, because

he Hiram was not Ulysses although Ulysses was his second name; because, and this is meant to tease, Hiram Ulysses Grant could from time
to time make a living. Which was not a mistake, not at all, not if it was
that. Remember Ulysses Simpson Grant never did make a living. Listen
to that.

Hiram Ulysses Grant was a leader in religion. He came every little
while neither to see nor to hear nor to wait, but just to manage to be
living might have made to earn a living. And because there is a camp-
meeting, in religion, and because there is religion in camp-meeting, he
had not any need to be there to be a leader in religion. Hiram Grant or
Hiram Ulysses Grant was a leader in religion.

What was Hiram Ulysses Grant before he changed.

He never had any other name than Hiram Grant or Ulysses Grant,
although they called him Sam. They called him, him Ulysses Simpson
Grant, Sam at West Point. This surprised me when I heard it. They
could not call him Saul because that was not in any way his name. But
then neither was Sam but they called him Sam just the same.

Perhaps they too had never been anywhere where they had heard
any one calling any one Hiram or Ulysses, and so Ulysses Simpson
making Uncle Sam they called him Sam. They would not have called
him Uncle Sam then because at that time he did not look like his own
or anybody else's uncle. He never did as a matter of fact. Later on he
was called United States' Grant not Uncle Sam's Grant. Anybody looking at his photograph would see why. He never did look like an uncle.
Sherman looked like an Uncle and they called him uncle, but not Grant,
no not Grant.

Whose name is Hiram. Whose name is Ulysses. Grant's name was
Hiram Grant's name was Ulysses, and why did they, do they, call him
Sam. Sam is short for Samson but this is not what they mean. Samuel
and Saul and all.

That was not what they meant. They meant U.S. or Uncle Sam
and you can also say US. us. This us, is what was said of us in this late
war, this that was the last, latest or greatest war. They said U.S. and
they said that meant us.

What is religion. Try again, what is religion. If he or you move slowly, that is religion. If you do not move at all. That is religion. Hiram Grant did neither move slowly nor at all. He was a leader in religion.

Religion is religion just the same.

They used to say very likely they still say, not of any one whose name everybody knows but of any one, Shame shame fie for shame, everybody knows his name. Nobody knows that they did and yet certainly they did at some time probably when he was very young young as is his habit say this to him of him. They made it capable of being him.

After all everybody knew his name, knows his name, and so he knew himself. He was Ulysses Simpson Grant, and so, not a leader in religion.

That is the way this is the way if you are a great man you discover that, you discover that you are a great man. Yes you do. You do do it just in that in this way.

There is another thing to know about religion and that is in respect to thanking. What is religion that is not when thanking. He thanks, he is religious, but he does say, I thank. This has perhaps nothing to do with either Hiram or Ulysses Grant, nor Sam Grant. It may not have anything to do with him. But it has something to do with around him. He does not, not any one of the three of them Hiram or Ulysses or Sam say I thank. For which he is not without or with them that is the others around him. He does not look so, no, not in his photograph.

He thanks and not only for a bird that is known to bring luck and money and came especially to say so, that is, I thank. He is not.

He Hiram Ulysses Grant did not thank. Not only. He not only thanks with, I thank.

Any one can remember this, in religion.

This has, I repeat it, nothing to do with Hiram Ulysses Grant, but it has to do with how to believe in what is religion. But not with him. And why. Because with him if he were to be a leader in religion religion is in a camp-meeting, and not, I thank.

Right back where we started from. Religion in a camp-meeting. There, there are no names, and religion. Nobody has to know any name. No not at all. And yet there are just those names, any names. Never forget a name and religion.

Religion is in a camp-meeting.

What is a camp-meeting.

How much this makes one think of what America was. Is America what it was. If I think so I say so.

A camp-meeting is a place where some one walks. And as some one walks they all kneel. And as they all kneel they all feel.

Nobody walks and talks, no not at a camp-meeting. If some one walks it follows that any one comes and this is a camp-meeting. They all cry and pray, they cry out loud or they cry with their eyes. Either one is just cries just the same as cries. Some one cries with their arm or their arms or their leg or their legs. Some cry with their eyes, their ears or their head. Some cry as if they were dead. Some cry with their ears instead. This is what they feel, this is what they kneel. This is what they know that even no name can tell them so. If when this you see remember me.

Did Ulysses Simpson Grant ever go to a camp-meeting. Did Hiram Ulysses Grant ever go to a camp-meeting. I rather do not think so or I do think so.

What do I know about religion. I know anything about religion. I know everything about religion. I know anything about American religion, but I do not know everything about Hiram Ulysses Grant being a leader in religion. Before I get through I will, I will know anything and everything and I will say everything about Hiram Ulysses Grant being a leader in religion.

And if I do not know everything and say everything about Grant being a leader in religion, I will say that I know everything and will say anything about American religion. I wonder if anything will escape me.

Hiram Ulysses Grant which he was born was he a leader in religion or was he not.

Volume II

Religion is not vexing in a camp-meeting, because whether seating, standing, walking, lying, or moving or mourning everything, that is to say, anybody is something and is doing something. The woods have nothing to do with it.

Might they the people not mind if they went away, that is if the woods went away. No they would not mind it at all. Not if the woods went away. Not if anything went away. Even if it went away to stay. They would not mind it anyway.

Hiram Ulysses Grant was a man who never meant to be told or kept, by not being here or yet. In that way could he mind if all the woods went away as well as any woods were not there to stay.

Religion is anxiously placing Grant before leaving. Come Grant, come away. Grant never comes away.

What is religion.

What is American religion.

Can in American religion any woods go away and stay. Is American religion placed on which they stay. Can American religion stay and go away. Can woods stay away or go away can American religion stay and not go away or say that the woods can stay and not if the woods can go away.

They do not mind if in a camp-meeting the woods can or do go away or are not there to stay.

Grant saw no one when he came and when he came he was not sitting, no, not Grant. Of course he could sit, but it was not the custom.

In some places it is the custom not to sit not to stand not to kneel and not to go away. In some places where anybody can stay just as if there was no place to stay not anybody can then not go away anyway. This is true of American religion, when they stay, if they go away. If the woods cannot stay not to go away. Oh yes they do now. Now if they are away they do or do not stay. That is the difference between now and then.

Grant was not ready, no if he was not ready, neither to stay, nor to go away, nor to wait, he was not a leader in religion. Hiram Grant was a leader in religion. If he had not been.

When is there religion, if he had not been. There always is religion.

It came to him to Hiram Ulysses Grant not as an easy thing but as a thing for which he was not waiting, to be a leader in religion. He was not waiting for anything.

No one, not any one is ever waiting. Not any one who never can or will or does or should or would earn a living.

And now I come to everything I have to say and what I have to say is this.

A real American a true American an American cannot earn a living. If he could earn a living he could be waiting. Waiting is what makes earning a living be a part of existing and succeeding. No American can succeed no American can earn a living. It is only because Americans are part European that they can earn a living because and this I cannot say too often because waiting is part of earning a living and there is no waiting in an American.

It seems so foolish that it is true that no American can earn a living that no American can succeed. Of course he cannot succeed, if he could succeed he could earn a living, and if he could earn a living he could wait. He cannot wait and therefore he cannot earn a living and therefore he cannot succeed. That is what you can call demonstrated or elucidated.

I like elucidating even better than demonstrating. Of course I do.

Success is not doing something, success is earning a living, and no good American can earn a living, he can make money but he cannot earn a living, not at all, not he, not he or as well she.

That is what I like. They say that an American can succeed but not at all not he. He can make money but not a living, not at all not he. When this you see remember me.

Hiram Grant might have made a living. Either Hiram or Ulysses or Hiram Ulysses or Ulysses Grant could not earn a living. Perhaps Hiram Grant might have, perhaps.

And the reason that an American cannot earn a living is that he is ready neither to stay nor to go away, nor to wait. Grant was not ready. He was ready neither to stay nor to go away, nor to wait, and so Hiram Grant was a leader in religion. If he had not been. If he had not been would there could there be religion. No of course not.

When is there religion.

There always is religion.

Hiram Ulysses Grant was a leader in religion every little while.

Was there religion American religion with their being certain that they could be there.

They never were there.

Of course they never were there.

No American ever was there. And yet there is American religion,

but American religion and that is where American differs from anybody else's religion has nothing whatever to do with anybody's being
or having been or going to be there. There which is anywhere.

Are you cute enough to see it, this, as well as feel it. I am.

And that is the difference. But Grant. Grant was not so different, as
he did or did not know, because neither he nor anybody else ever told
anybody else so.

Volume III

HIRAM ULYSSES GRANT never fell away from his name but Ulysses
Simpson Grant was not the same.

Hiram Ulysses Grant has now gotten to be so different from Ulysses
Simpson Grant that they could not even have been born brothers. I my-
self prefer Ulysses Simpson Grant but he had less initiative than Hiram
Ulysses Grant and less of a certain kind of force. What is in a name.
Now you know. Everything is in a name. Character and career.

They were neither of them, remember they were not related, they
were neither of them by nature really concerned with camp-meetings,
although either or both of them had been to them. They have been sometimes, as well as quite often.

Do you begin to see how different they are each one of them from the
other one.

Grant, that is Ulysses Simpson Grant was not ready, he was not
ready. Neither would he stay, nor go away, nor wait.

And so Hiram Ulysses Grant was a leader in religion. If he had not
been.

This being a leader in religion came to Hiram Ulysses Grant not as
an easy thing, but as a thing for which he was not waiting. You see in
that respect the two of them are alike. Neither one was waiting for anything. No one, not any one of either one of them is ever waiting.

Hiram Ulysses Grant every little while was not waiting, and at any
rate no one could dispute anything. He was a leader in religion. He
came every little while neither to see nor to hear nor to wait, but just to
manage to be living that is making a living, that is earning his living.
And because there is camp-meeting in religion and because there is re-

ligion in camp-meeting, he had not any need to be a leader in religion. Hiram Grant or Hiram Ulysses Grant was a leader in religion.

Now about Ulysses Simpson Grant, if you said all these things again they would sound the same but they would be very different. He was going to be a leader in war and that although it looks and acts the same is different. Pretty soon I will explain why American religion and American war are different and not the same. And yet already you begin to see it as well as feel it. You begin to see just by their name that Hiram Ulysses Grant and Ulysses Simpson Grant are not the same. This is the power of a name and a name is in war and a name is in religion. It is not the same name, and the name is not the same. Not in the way they see it which is just later what they see, that is the same as feel it.

Ulysses Simpson Grant one could not pin him down as to why Grant was here. He had not meant to ascertain that he was there. Not if he was to be a leader in war which is not the same as a leader in religion even if it does look as if it could and would be the same. Anybody can begin to see what now is in a name.

Ulysses Simpson Grant was there as often as he came but he never came. That makes war later all the same.

Religion is much as it was but not all. Much as it was means that they believed if they did. But not all by all means, that there is something else. How can any one say they would come, but now, they would come. This cannot be said in a word. This is or is not a camp-meeting. Think of Grant Hiram Grant leading in religion. He was quiet as he forgot not to lead in religion. Quiet is like waiting. There is no such thing not for any one not for any one or for him. Not at all. He was not favored to wait, and not favored not to help not leading in religion. He led in religion. Of course he did.

Now think how different it is in war. Ulysses Simpson Grant was not favored to wait and he in a way went away. But later as they came not to wait and he was not waiting, one of two, how well they knew they who are not one of two, that no one will come. Well and waiting for no one of two. Do you see what I mean. Or no this will not do but he was not one of two.

Ulysses Simpson Grant did not feel differently but he was not surrounded by himself differently. That is the way it is. Surround and around are two different words and if nobody is waiting that which is this is American war. Do you see what I mean.

As surround and around are two different words, surround has nothing to do with surrender, around has nothing to do with surrender. No not in an American war. Do you see how different any other words are. And they are just as they are either so or not so.

Ulysses Simpson Grant did not feel differently from any one of one of two. This is what I mean and this will do. He was not surrounded by himself differently, this which makes no difference. It makes no difference not if there are one of two. By this I mean just this. Some surround themselves by themselves differently even if they are one of two and three. But not he. Not even he when he was by himself alone.

I mean, in American war, there are as many as if there was no war. And at the same time Ulysses Simpson Grant was not surrounded by himself differently because in an American war there are not one of two. There are not one of two any more nor even more in any American war. Not any more than if nobody has any part of any more.

Do you see what I mean by this. Yes.

In an American war, nobody can dream because if you dream you wait just as much as a dream. And so they know how not, not there. But really not, because it could be not a dream. It could not be a dream and so no dream can seem to be a dream, not it. No no no American religion no American war is there. There is a place, dream is a place and there is no place there there where American war or American religion can be there. Oh.

Religion is much as it was but not all. Much as it was means they believed if they did, but not by all means that there is something else.

That is what makes no more of an American war than if there was more there. In religion in American religion also there is as if it was that is if there was more there. But in an American war in American religion there is no place there. That makes it that there is no way for them to cry or to try, not for them. One should never tell them what they cannot do.

How can any one say they would come, but now, they would come.

This can only be said in a word. But there is no word. There is no word in American religion in American war, there is no word there.

Remember this but not at all no one can call out if they remember, no one can not call out if they remember.

They need not remember to be an American war or any more. They need not remember to be an American religion any member.

Hiram Ulysses Grant and call out, think again of not or not. Of course not. Of course no American can call out. No of course not.

Ulysses Simpson Grant and call out, why not if there is no not. Of course not.

But which was not only not prepared but all of it in places. There is never any please in places. I mean there is please in places but not in American religion or in American war.

This is or is not a camp-meeting. Think of Grant, Hiram Grant leading in religion. He was quiet as he forgot not to lead in religion. He led in religion. Of course he did.

It makes no difference if it is true that Hiram Grant led. No difference at all. No one waited while he led and no one has to wait. That is the way they like it that religion is led while they wait. But they do not wait. It is interesting if it is true that they do. They do. They do not wait, this is true, even if there is American religion in them all through.

It is easy to think of Hiram Grant not waiting, very easy. It is just as very easy to think of no one waiting. No one waits. Cannot you understand that. And what is religion, American religion, it has nothing to do with just that.

Come and come and no one calls at all. In other places any one can call. But not in American religion, almost not in American war at all.

Call. There are so many things no one does not do in American religion not in American war not at all. Not because they do not but because it is not, oh not at all, not ever could or would, no not as much as any part of all.

There is in American religion there is in American war no part of all, no part of all at all.

Do you see. Cecile do you see or Nellie or Sophy. Do any of you see anything at all. If you do you know as well as ever that there never is any part of all. Now some can learn to see but not American war not American religion, not American at all.

What I wish to say is this, in any way there could be a part of all but not in American religion not in American war.

Now just think of this a moment. You know that Ulysses Simpson Grant could not be any part of all. But of course not. Anybody can see what is not, but there, there is nothing to see at all, because in Ulysses Simpson Grant there is no part of all. Do you see now why American is what it is. I hope so.

On the other hand Hiram Grant is not part of all at all but as he was he was not any part of all. And that made no difference because after all he had no wish. Thousands millions have no wish, which is it.

Hiram Grant, you can see already that we now have them.

Hiram Grant.

Hiram Ulysses Grant.

Ulysses Simpson Grant.

Hiram Grant is not interesting, he could earn a living perhaps before he lost it. At any rate he was not a leader he was not a leader in religion he was not a leader in war at all.

Hiram Ulysses Grant is a leader in religion although many would not be alike. Nobody is alike not only with him but without him.

Hiram Ulysses Grant could not be known. He was there.

Hiram Grant was a leader in religion Ulysses Simpson Grant the same Grant. Grant was a leader in religion. No one knew him. No one knew how.

Did Grant mind how he liked religion, did he ask how it ended.

Did he know that it did not only end but that it ended like that. Grant, Hiram Ulysses Grant, did you know, did you know that it was like that, that it did not stop, that there is a difference between ending and stopping, oh Grant tell us Grant did you know that.

Of course he knew that. If he did not know that what did he know.

Oh Grant how do you like being a leader in religion, Hiram Ulysses Grant how do you like being a leader in religion. Come and say how you do like being a leader in religion. They cannot answer to say, no not they, not one of one in any way.

To begin again out loud. Hiram U. Grant never did or could begin out loud. Of course not.

One at a time. It is funny how three make a crowd out loud when there is only one. It is not even one, one, one.

One at a time Hiram Ulysses Grant was a leader in religion.

Now what is the difference. Do you really have to say anything to be a leader in religion in American religion or do you not. Is it necessary to speak. Who can speak. Not an American even in religion but yes of course an American in religion. He can speak or he can speak. Nobody speaks which nobody misses now.

There are no names in American religion, no names now.

Hiram. Ulysses Grant was a leader in religion. He had no way to hesitate to say that as it went on it was a way, not to wait, until it would be only the way, not in the way. They like what they infer.

Think of all the leaders of religion American religion, and how different they are from all the leaders in religion. They had not a way to hesitate to say that it went on in a way, that was not to wait until it would be the only way. No waiting. Do you not see there is no waiting. And so how religion changes that is American religion.

Do you see how Hiram Ulysses is not the same as just religion and Grant is like that, was like it. A name. And yet there is no name in American religion all the same there is no name, no names. He was a leader in religion.

He had no way to hesitate to say that as it went on it was a way not to wait until it would be only the way. Do you see the difference between only the way and the only way. Everybody does say.

Now just think everybody think of the difference between Hiram Ulysses Grant and Ulysses Simpson Grant. You begin to see the difference. But of course you do.

Ulysses Simpson when he came to be a leader in war was not at all any more and he never was differently himself around him, that is to say and it is now not too late to say that he had no way to hesitate to say that as it went on it was a way not to wait until it would be only the way.

He never waited to be in the way. Do you see now how there is no wait-ing in American war.

And now do you see this just is not Ulysses Simpson Grant. It is not Ulysses Simpson Grant at all. It is Hiram Ulysses Grant. Do you not see that.

Ulysses Simpson Grant had no way no way at all and nothing went on as it went on and there was no way. He did not say which way was in a word he did not say there was no word. Hesitate and wait, they are words two words, one word or any word. There could not be in Ulysses Simpson Grant only the way because in an American war there is no way at all, not a way not a place not a place to go or stay.

And remember just as many anyway as if there was no war at all.

American war, do not go away, Ulysses Simpson Grant not to come or stay or go away or hesitate to state because there is no state unless there are all the states there, there just as yet.

By this I mean that American religion and American war is not the same. I mean. Hiram Ulysses Grant and Ulysses Simpson Grant are not the same. One is in religion, one in war but neither one can be one any more not any more because neither one is one of two. So think of each one.

Think in the way they think.

What happened to him first.

They called him Sam but that was not his name, but after any while, any name can come to be the name they mean when they called him Sam. Sam Grant. That is naturally mine. Nobody says it but it is like it. He never went away at all from any name, not Sam, not Hiram not Ulysses, not Simpson not Grant.

What is a name. What is religion what is war. What is anything any more.

Grant forgot he had any other name and then it comes to be that no one knows how very likely he looked as he was. He did not look around for it a name.

He had a life he had a wife he had a boy he had his clothes he had a horse but that is not worth while because he could walk, and he had a camp stool upon which he sat. This can be seen in any photograph.

There was an American war. Just as much an American war as when there is, that it is, where they come and they do not come, where they were there where they were, not there where they meant. They did not mean where they will, they cannot will. It would mean that they would write a will which they did not. Of course why they did not.

Can you see an American war, there is no use of saying an American war with or without U. S. Grant. That makes no use of yes or success. Not at all. An American war and I cannot say too often that in an American war there are as many there as if there was no war at all, in an American war there is no there, there is no where, there is no addition or subtraction but there is elucidation and left left left right left quickly spoken.

And there is no will, nobody makes a will, no not in an American war.

Oh why oh why do they wish a wish is. They never wish. They can never wish. They can never will because to will you must be dead to will, of course. To wish, you must will to wish, and so they cannot if they were to wish.

Oh say can you see what I say.

In an American war they went where they went to the war but they went that is no one went. What is went. Went is to go and nobody can say no or go. Not in an American war.

And now in an American war there is no use for Grant but Grant is there U. S. Grant is there. Where is Grant. Not there. Where is an American war, not there. An American war, Grant U. S. Grant, not at all why they were with or without each.

Once upon a time there was a big American war. Everybody was an American war and there is nobody who is not met to be yet. Yet there always is an American war. The paper says no more American war and underneath it says they did it yet. Yet. Grant was not ready yet.

I often wonder if a little while they know they really place to-day, that they will call a name a name any day. Ulysses Simpson Grant is foolish. Grant. Sam Grant. Photographed Grant. Wet Grant. Yet Grant. Can you see how it follows the sound. The same follows the sound or is with it just there yet.

Volume IV

ANOTHER subject.

What is religion.

Religion is this. They act as in religion that is to say they neither wait nor stay away. Religion is best as it is. If they like it at all they like it all, not only more than once but often.

Interesting if true.

Is American religion just like that. Is American religion best as it is and do they act, that is to say they neither wait nor stay away.

Think of a camp-meeting, can you say that they neither wait nor stay away. Perhaps yes.

Is American religion best as it is. Do you think of a camp-meeting and say yes. Yes as it is.

In American religion if they like it at all they like it all, is that so.

In American religion is it not only more than once but often, think of an American camp-meeting think of it. Think that it makes no difference if the words are not words and the trees are not trees and the camp-meeting is not a camp-meeting, think if it makes any difference in American religion.

There is American religion never the less.

Volume V

WHAT do you imagine of religion. Grant never asked any one about anything and this can make a religion.

It is very likely that they like that missionaries can like to have a house all covered with all kinds of postage stamps and each time they do it a little child is given to them, just for ordinary stamps, the kind with which letters are sent.

Grant did know something of this, as did she who was pious and he who was married. Grant did not add anything but he knew.

Did it matter to Grant. Yes anything mattered to Grant which he did not hear which he did not see. As granted. This sounds funny but it is not. As granted.

Anything mattered to Grant. Grant to Grant. Like Grant. As Grant.
Let me describe Grant and religion.

Which Grant.

Grant.

As can Grant can can Grant a soldier be.

If there are no soldiers between them.

Of course not, if of course not, why not.

The twentieth century following the nineteenth century found out
why not.

The eighteenth century knew that soldiers were soldiers that is to
say they were different from others.

The nineteenth century said soldiers were soldiers but after all
soldiers were men.

And we, U.S. we, us, in the nineteenth century discovered the
twentieth century because we discovered there were no such thing as
soldiers even in a war. Everybody knew it in the beginning of the nineteenth century and then they forgot it and then in the middle of all that
forgetting in the middle of the nineteenth century we the U.S. knew it
even in a big war. And this will lead me to say so many things later
about war, funny things really things about war.

The funny things I wish to say about war is first how war only says
what everybody knows.

Everybody likes to see pictures, pictures of what everybody knows.
Pictures of what everybody knows that that is a war.

Everybody knows which side has won before there is a war, everybody knows it, but nobody likes to believe it, and then they make a
war. Dogs bark, that is war, but they all already know some one was
coming.

Everybody knows what most everybody knew, but now to show it
they make a war and after the war is over they believe it. The real fighting has all always been done before the war commences but as everybody likes explanations everybody likes everything proved everybody
likes a war so there has to be the war. Think of any war. Of course what
I say is true. The war is always won before the war, of course of course.
Anybody knows that.

Now why do you say you do not want war. Of course you do want war because this is a way of seeing when you look and we like to look oh yes we like to look. Show me I'm from Missouri and that is war. He from Missouri knows but he wants to be shown and that is war. And why not. Most everybody wants to be shown. And that is war.

And so we in the nineteenth century discovered there were no such things as soldiers. Men fought or did not fight, mostly they did mostly they do. Mostly they do not mostly they did not. Oh yes you too.

There is no such thing as war there is no such thing as soldiers, but men fight, why, because they do. And as they do it for. Or for. Of course for.

And so do you see why.

Do you begin to see why. There is a war. Always is a war. Always is even is an American war.

Let me describe Grant and religion. What would Grant Hiram Ulysses Grant or Ulysses Simpson Grant have done if he had been a great religious leader.

But not in for a war. The reason that Grant could fight in an American war was because he was one to be one to have it that this was so that the American war was won before there was the war. But the war oh yes the war was or was to be there, not where not anywhere.

You see Sherman said war was hell that was because he was fighting a war, but Grant he was a leader in an American war and the war was not where, where was the war. If not why not.

Because in anyway there was no there, there where there was any or a war. There were just as many there there which is where, there is or was or is no more or was no war.

Do you begin to see, the real Ulysses Simpson Grant he knew there was no war. There is always fighting but there is no war. And why because any why is neither my or not my it is all over before.

A war is over before there is the war. Do you begin to see that.

Of course it is all over before. It always is and this is any war which war.

Do you begin to say why Ulysses Simpson Grant was in an American war.

And that Hiram Ulysses Grant was different, that he was in American religion.

Do you begin to see. Oh yes you begin to see.

Chapter III

DOES what Hiram Ulysses Grant does have anything to do with religion. No I do not think so nor do I think does he. Grant does not think so he does not did not think that what he did has anything to do with religion, nor either what he is or was.

Therefore it is not necessary to tell what he did, nor is it at all necessary to tell what he is or was.

It is necessary to know his name. No one knows but me how necessary it is to know his name. Now think how it came or even if you please how it comes.

You will never have known a Hiram and then in one summer you will know three. Or make believe it is Mariuses. You have never known a Marius and in a summer there are three. An Italian Marius a french Marius and a Swiss Marius, and so do you see what it is to have a name all the same. Hiram is a name Ulysses is a name even though there never has come to be one here of that name. And then comes one, often then the other one, then there are three. Will you be.

Have any of you noticed this.

By this I mean just this. That anybody may forget a name. Therefore it is not necessary to tell what he did, nor is it either at all necessary to tell what he is or was.

It is necessary to tell what is religion.

It is necessary to tell what Grant could have done if he had been a saint or a leader in religion. There is no need at all to know what he does or did or what he was or is.

It is necessary if you have a name to be in a way behaving with a name. Hiram Ulysses Simpson Grant. No Hiram Grant. Ulysses Simpson Grant. You see I have lost a name. Between them they have lost a name. They will not lose their name not all the same. They do, some do, lose some name.

In American they often just like that change their name. Not because of their profession as in other countries but just because they do like it like that. Sometimes they say there is a reason.

For this it is necessary to know what is religion. Just as necessary to know this as to know your name so that you can come when you are called. No one can lose religion American religion any more than anybody can lose one name. Not only their name but any name. Do you feel like that.

It is very necessary any name is very necessary, it is necessary because of religion and yet in American religion they do not need any name all the same they do not need any name.

It is necessary because of Hiram Ulysses Grant who does not interest us.

It is necessary because of religion which does interest us. Because of Hiram Grant who does interest us.

It is necessary because of Ulysses Simpson Grant who does interest us and who may or who may not have known anything of religion. But he did. No American can not know about American religion. There is no no in place. Do you see what I mean. There is no no in American religion. Do you see what I mean.

If he had been a religious leader or a saint what would he have done to have been one.

But first let us know what is religion. If we can, let us know what is American in religion.

Not to lose a name that is not to forget to name any one with a name. They cannot help it. As soon as they come they come with a name. But they do not need a name.

Call a name and not need a name that, that is American religion.

Now see, see that you see that to lose and to forget is not the same, neither if it is done with or without a name.

American religion.

I like it.

American religion there are no favours to forget nor names.

American religion is not prepared, they need not ask anxiously, there is no anxiety in American religion not one.

Nor either is there wind nor a window no not in American religion.

There is no thanks or welcome no not in an American religion.

There is no sky, no there is no sky. And why. For the very simple reason that there is no sky, not in American not in American religion and why. Why is there no sky.

And so you see why American religion and European religion have nothing in common. Nothing at all.

European religion has a sky.

So heaven is there on high.

American religion has no sky and why. Because America has no sky. And why. Because that is why. There is only air and no sky. That is why.

Each one is all.

In American religion there is no one, there is no part of all, there is no sky, and why. Why. Because there is no sky. No one is shy, why, because there there is no sky.

A sky is a thing seen when you look up, when you look up in America you see up. That is all.

Do you see now what I mean by wind and windows.

You see in European religion they need a wind and they need window but not I, not American religion, not I. They need no wind or window or sky because there is no wind no window and no sky, not in American religion not in American war, not in America before or after war.

Wind has nothing to do with American religion. If there is no sky there is no wind to by and by, and so American religion is not why. Why not.

Do you see they know no moon nor sun nor stars nor bars but which they will not in their American religion.

Do you begin to see now why American religion will, there is no will be still, no not in American religion.

Sometime you come along. But not without the game of a name. Not not without the same game of the same name.

The name is this.

It does not make any difference when they come if they know that their name is so and so. But this does not savour of religion or make let a dog into a garden.

An American religion.

Do you often feel like this in an American religion.

I thought that I could think that I would not care to say what he had done and what he could do. And yet perhaps it is better to do so.

Remember he was born and changed his name because it was done for him.

We are still talking about Grant.

Remember also that he had been called Sam and this was done for him. Also remember that any one can seem to be the only one. That is to say it is remarkable how often you think that any one is an only child.

Ulysses Simpson Grant was or was not an only child but he had had to be one of some one.

Might that be religion American religion. That anybody might be a child if not an only child of some one. Think every minute if that might not be religion American religion that any one could be an only child or of some one or more than so.

As much as he could know of how to go. I think religion can be so.

And now I know it makes no difference whether his name was Hiram Ulysses or Ulysses Simpson although I really know that it does and did.

When anybody becomes a saint they change their name and so it must make a great deal of difference.

What is religion American religion. He never asks.

Hiram Ulysses Grant met no one that is to say it was not his way to meet any one because meeting any one is an occupation and he had no interest in any occupation.

That is the way it was. He had no interest, that is the way it was.

There is no way of having any interest in religion in American religion. That is the way it was.

And what has this to do with American religion. Not anything in one way.

To occupy anything or to be occupied makes it as if it is occupied by something and this was not what he had to do. Not at all. He had not that to do. Not at all.

He was a leader in religion in American religion.

May she may he call wood and hay wood and hay.

But he did not have to say either or both as a way to pray. Prayer is not necessary in religion in American religion. What to say.

What to say.

Now think of solemn and sky.

They both begin with s and mean the same only one is in American religion and the other not.

Solemn is in American religion because being in American religion an only child in which there is no sky and no die one must be solemn. If one is not solemn one is not an only child and with no sky, but American religion is, it is an only child and with no sky and with no die. You may be killed but not to die not I an only child cannot die, it can be solemn it can lie it can be killed, but it cannot die and why because an only child can not die. That is why.

Do you begin to see a little what America is what American religion is what American war is.

Do you see what it is. Lizzie do you see.

Do you see what American religion is and why there is no sky. Every where else there is a sky and why because the sky is over all. But in American religion there is no sky because there is no over all. There is no all, there is no over all. That is why.

So that is the difference between solemn and sky.

You say you do not like me to repeat but why not if it makes you listen.

And it will make you listen does make you listen. You like the funny things in the newspapers because they repeat, why yes of course you do.

I say why not if it makes you listen.

Now you see American religion is solemn but it is not an all nor an over all nor is it any part of all not at all.

Hiram Ulysses Grant just then popped into my mind. I knew just what he was when he was standing and not slouching also the way he was dressed and what he said. What did he say. They listened but they did not hear what he had to say, what he said. He said it again but they did not hear again. That is what I call right.

Hiram Ulysses Grant never made them yet, only not yet, nor that he will.

He was a leader in religion although he never meant well never meant them well, not yet.

He may not say that he was not to answer because he did not hear. Not at all not at all there was nothing to hear because as he had ears he did not hear.

Any and all of this is an occupation and there is no danger in religion no danger in American religion.

There is no danger in religion is there any danger in war, some say not. Safety first has nothing to do with danger and so I tell you no there is no danger in American religion nor in American war nor in America, no no danger.

By this I mean that where anybody can be killed there is no danger. Because being killed is so easy there and so nobody is in danger.

There is danger in an occupation, danger in occupation, because if anything is occupying then good-bye to religion, if not good-bye to war any more, any way good-bye to religion, good-bye to anything, oh yes oh yes, good-bye.

Arrange religion as not an occupation.

Once more he comes Hiram Ulysses Grant comes and he does not resemble Grant. If not why not why does he not resemble him at all at all, not resemble Ulysses Simpson Grant, not at all, not at all, at all.

He is heavier and thinner, he is taller and yellower, he is older and redder he is a leader. Nobody comes when he calls.

He wears a beard, perhaps he is drunk every day perhaps, perhaps he needs where he goes if not, perhaps, who thinks of wills and willing or moon and sun and is he willing. He is not willing to stop and he is not willing except when he is working and he never shakes a hand not when he is willing. He is willing to come alone, or not.

That is what he is not, willing.

Hiram Ulysses Grant is a leader in religion if he is willing. Do you see how different he is from Ulysses Simpson Grant whom you all know by his photograph. Of course you do of course you see how different he is. One in war and one in religion. And who knows the difference. Because after all who can say that there is any any day either war, or either religion, or either, not at all.

Arrange religion as not an occupation. Neither is war. That is the reason why everybody anybody can like it. Of course that is a reason if not the reason. Yes of course. It not being an occupation anybody can like it.

There you are, believe it or not, there is no occupation that can be what it is.

I cannot feel that they declare that Grant was there. Of course he was there.

Which Grant.

Why can religion be a farewell to when they come. Which Grant.

Not at all. In religion they do not come and so Grant never said good-bye.

Which Grant never said good-bye. Neither one nor the other Grant ever said good-bye. Of course not. Think of that. Think of an American at that. They never said good-bye. Not one. Which Grant. No Grant, no Grant ever said good-bye.

In religion they do not stay and so Grant never said anything.

Have you forgotten the way Grant looked.

Which Grant.

Have you forgotten what he never did. Have you forgotten what he never said. Have you forgotten. Which Grant.

Grant had no occupation. He did not do that.

How often they say not but no Grant ever said not. Of course not. Think of the two not as Grant but as each one.

Hiram U. Grant was a leader in religion. Nobody said anything. He did not do anything but he had an occupation. Which one. Which did he have as an occupation.

In religion they do not wait and so Grant had no ocupation.

In religion they leave nothing and so Grant never went away.

I know what Hiram U. Grant looks like I know what he says I know what he does I know where he lives I know what he likes I know how he works I know how he drinks and I know how he shakes hands. Yes I do. Because I can see him any day spring summer and autumn not winter. I cannot see him when winter comes. And why. Because when winter comes there is no way to say that he is there. But he is just as much as yes.

And so you see religion has this use that if he led in religion which he did he not only did not come and go or stay and wait or speak or leave. Not at all.

He was a leader in religion. Remember that. Everybody remember that. Hiram Ulysses Grant was a leader in religion. Remember that. A leader in American religion remember that. Not a leader in french religion. He was a leader in American religion. Remember that.

Ulysses Simpson Grant, remember, that was Grant.

Remember that he was Grant.

I do not care very much to know that he was called Sam Grant. This can be such a disappointment that as well as so I do not wish to know but I do know that once he was called Sam Grant. I find this useless.

Now to come back to Hiram Ulysses. He was drunk, he was drunk every day and all day and did or did this not make any difference. It did not. And why not. Because if he was drunk all day and every day and every bit of every day it did not make any difference.

He began every day as if it was all finished at the end of any other day. Which it was in his life time. It was all finished. In his life time.

He could be known not to be left alone because as he stood there, although he never stood, he was always as it were never left where any one could stare. Not he. He was never there. He could be accompanying what ever needed to be used that day, hay, beasts, land, help, grain, barns or wood, just as they know they would.

This made him be left alone to-day. No one can say he could be left alone to-day or any day.

He was a leader in religion not which they or any one can say. If he were big and thin and tall and all and always well as drunk as when he was no longer well. Who could call who around. Do you not hear around when practically nothing else is said or set.

For which they please to come.

What do they ask for.

They ask for nothing.

He never said that of any one not of any one who had nothing to do. He never said it.

He liked their allowance when he gave them enough.

They were best anywhere.

In all their ages they were none of them all. Or even at all.

A leader in religion has a wife. He has to have a wife who listens and believes and minds. Of course she does. She never knew who or to whom.

She will prefer her eldest son to her youngest and her youngest son to her eldest. But this is alright.

By which they mean they are not restless because it has to have a habit that well is well. They know they prefer where they mean. She felt it best. That is to say she felt that it was what it was best. She did it too. Every little while to try.

To lead in religion in American religion means that cakes are plain. Of course they are. Anybody knows that. They are plain. Those who have the occasion know where they go. The other way to say the same thing is to say. Cakes are not plain neither birds or beasts. And as we can say. Or quite likely they will not be frightened not while they are alike. Not while cakes are alike.

I lose myself in thoughts. Who does not who knows the difference between drunken and cakes. Not drunken because never without drink, not cakes because never without cakes. Not tall because never without all. Not pursued because well what is it without. Not what is it without withered. You tell me if you have no variation.

I think how likely Hiram Ulysses Grant looked just like I think he did.

Book 14

Now to tell a story simply.

What is religion and why was Hiram Ulysses Grant a religious leader.

If nobody told him and nobody did tell him, how did he know.

Hiram did not tell any one so, but they did know.

Just how they knew is not why they were not through with him, or any one.

American religion cannot make anybody tell any one any more, or anything about that thing.

See him not tell any one anything about anything that has been anything of that thing.

Nobody tells any one anything about seeing anything, not in American religion or any such thing.

And so Hiram Ulysses Grant could be a leader in American religion do you begin to see that, although he was never leading. No one in any American thing is leading anything. With anything anything is any thing. So that is the way that there is nothing leading or anything following which is that thing.

They act as if they all go together one by one and so any one is not leading. Do you see that in American religion in American anything.

Just as if that which nobody did tell him was not something he did not do.

Do you want a story do you want to know everything about what he did not do. Why yes.

What is religion.

Religion is, that if they said this, they had that.

Not for him or from him not him.

Hiram Ulysses Grant had not that kind of American religion. Not with him. He had no kind of religion with him. Not Hiram Ulysses Grant.

You now never could mix up the two could you.

Hiram told no one anything and he heard nothing when he told no one anything. And that amounted to that. Believe him if you can.

Not for him.

Not for Hiram Ulysses Grant, not for him.

It might, it should it might amount to that. That Hiram Ulysses Grant was a leader in religion.

Just like that, just what he meant by what was said. He did not say anything.

Do you remember how I said he was well, what he said, do you remember how I said he did not say anything. He was just the way he looked. His head, his beard, he was drunk but he was not said, because it was all always there, there was never anything.

Oh yes he was as he said but he did not say it as they said. He did not say anything.

All of which was meant.

There is no such thing as wounds or wounded, no such thing.

There is no such thing as first and all the time. No there is no such thing.

Hiram Ulysses Grant did not have to know that there was such a thing he did not have to know.

Why should Hiram Ulysses Grant be last. Nobody said last nobody said lost. Nobody said lost or last. Nobody said at last.

Hiram Ulysses Grant did not have to know that there was not any such a thing he did not have to know.

Oh no, no he did not have to know.

Did you begin to see how religion well he is a leader in religion I say he.

Let me tell you about Hiram Ulysses Grant. He had a father he was taller older and more bearded but he was never what he need not be not he. He looked like that. He looked like a leader in religion but it was not he because he did not have to be not he.

Hiram Ulysses Grant married his cousin, he did this to please his father and he and his wife had two sons one older and one younger.

This was not to please any father but never more than earlier and later it did please any and even every father.

This was what Hiram Ulysses Grant saw.

Later he was always better than rather, further than farther and ready to be in after he could not deny any farther.

And then he was not drunk but never sober. This did not interfere with anything so indeed it did not.

This was how he was a religious leader not any one was any farther not any one further not any one follow or fear nearer. Just not it.

Then they all know that Hiram Ulysses Grant was not so too.

They knew he was new.

Oh yes. New.

Volume VI

ULYSSES SIMPSON GRANT was the general in the civil war in the United States of America.

He was not as stout or as heavy or as dark or as broad a man as one might think.

He was paler and smaller and lighter and shorter and narrower than might have been thought.

This could come to be a fact.

But he was a leader in religion.

Is that so.

No.

Not he nor his brother but Hiram Ulysses Grant. Oh yes of course.

Ulysses Simpson Grant was after all there.

Of course he was there and he gathered it all together, all all together and he did not cry about it, some leaders in religion have wept. Very often.

Some leaders in war.

Have not cried about it at all.

Neither Grant led.

They did not cry nor try.

May they cry as they try.

Some leaders can.

Volume VII

ULYSSES SIMPSON GRANT never kept when he wept. Or why should he try and cry. Not he.

The whole thing about Ulysses Simpson Grant beside that he did not earn a living was that he did not. One man did say, did not, about anything and really nobody did say did, about anything. He did not say anything.

He was not after which they settled. By this I mean he did not look to see anything. He never said I mean. He had a son too, two sons if he had two. There might have been girls too but not if they went without.

They can shoot if they have a gun and if they have none, they can shoot too. Yes they do. It is easy to eat what is shot. It is easy if better not. Who has been without any one. This was not Ulysses Simpson Grant's past.

He never had a present. They may just as well say why not as not say why not. But he did not place himself any where. Which is just the same as all the same.

It is not often that it is only cold in winter. It is better. That which they have is better. Any day they have what they have eaten. Some say cooked and eaten. Some say not.

I wish I remembered everything about Ulysses S. Grant. But I do. Why should I look as I do if I do.

I remember everything about Grant Ulysses S. Grant just as anybody can do.

I can lose Ulysses S. Grant and in a way I have having made him another having made Hiram Ulysses Grant. I have made him Hiram U. Grant.

Volume VIII

WHAT is religion and why could Hiram Grant be a leader in religion as he was.

This is the way to lead religion.

In the first place neither he nor they must be ready.

They must none of them be ready at all.

They must none of them have been waiting and they must none of them have been prepared to go anywhere.

They must not merely not hear but not lead.

They must also not despair nor place any one anywhere.

In this way religion is bound to be born by not being either frightened or alone.

Not anything can happen to any one.

And so religion is partly mine.

So do you see Hiram Ulysses Grant was not a parent, nor had he no children, nor had he any intention of moving. None of these things occurred to him.

He could be known not to have known about religion.

Does he begin.

Do you begin.

Will they begin.

May he begin. Which way should never be said by any one for him.

When this you see see me or him.

This makes which makes that they make religion.

What is religion.

Religion is in return for their religion.

Do you read led for religion.

In this way nobody led.

Hiram Ulysses Grant led in religion.

Grant was a leader in religion.

To come back to Ulysses Simpson Grant and what he did and what he did do and what he was. And was Hiram Ulysses Grant a leader in religion. He was. I cannot ask too often what is religion.

That is what they do. Who do.

That is what they do. They do ask who asks what is religion. They do not ask what is religion but I do. I ask what is religion. I cannot ask too often, what is religion.

What is religion.

Religion is what is alright if they have to have their ups and downs. It is also alright if everything remains the same, it is also alright if there is a leader in religion. It is also alright. But who is. Who is alright.

So often as I say so often as I think so often as I can I say when is American religion not for a man not for a woman not for children. When is it and when is it not. When is it religion and when is it not.

It is always religion.

American religion is always religion.

What is religion.

Religion is made of which so many not only come at once but come more than just at once. Remember the camp-meeting and that it would make no difference if the woods went away to stay, just this.

If they came at once it would be just that. But if they came at once would there be a leader in religion.

Think everybody think. Which is Hiram Ulysses Simpson Grant. Which did he not hear to do. Which.

Think of Hiram Ulysses Grant. Yes because they have heard nothing of who said anything and no one spoke.

Is this so. Or is this not true.

After they went together.

Hiram was not like that, he not only remained but he came after a while and he did not come at all because as no one waited there was no way for him to move.

Think about it all.

No one can move.

Oh no. No one can move.

If no one can wait and no one can move and this is so if you think about it that is to say if you know what you know you do know that this is so.

Not at all.

No one can wait.

There is no such thing as waiting.

Volume IX

No ONE sent for Ulysses Simpson Grant no one indeed. No indeed. Not at all while anybody went.

No one sent, listen to this, no one sent for Ulysses Simpson Grant as long that is while anybody went.

He could remember that he did not feel that he was sad and never had been.

Is this Ulysses Simpson. Yes it is Ulysses Simpson.

Is this Hiram Ulysses.

Well yes perhaps it is.

Hiram U. Grant was a leader in religion.

There is no more sadness in religion than there is waiting. In American religion in any American religion.

No more welcome in religion than there is moving. That is in religion in American religion in American religion.

I do not repeat what I say, I say what I say and that sounds like the same thing, and it is, and why not if the same thing is which it is. And yet it is not, not the same thing, and so it is that is so it happens that I do not say what I have said. I keep saying what it is that I have to say. I say it about religion American religion about American war even about American everything. Yes I do.

He was not welcome he did not welcome.

There is no welcome in religion.

No more welcome in religion than there is moving.

And why did he not sit and think.

He neither sat nor thought.

He neither walked nor bought.

There is no sitting and thinking in religion.

Not in American religion.

There is no walking or buying in religion. Not in American religion.

What is there in religion.

Hiram Ulysses Grant was a leader in religion.

But which I know if all I say I do, but this has nothing else to do with you.

This has nothing to do with it, even if as a wish, he says to his brother you talk like a fish.

All this could be heard out loud but Hiram Ulysses Simpson was not there. Why not. Because if no one was, it was not as if no one was.

Do you feel them clear or clearly.

Can you see the Grants like this Hiram Ulysses Simpson but they were not both brothers. One can be a brother the other can be a brother but not two of one of them no not two of them can be the brother.

How could I know if I were to say so that there is a difference between Hiram Ulysses Grant and Ulysses Simpson Grant.

Who was Grant.

Grant what he would be doing what would he be doing if instead of a general he had been a leader in religion.

What would he be doing if instead of being a leader in religion he had been a general.

And how old is the difference.

Volume X

FORGET how many generals there are in the world and how many leaders in religion.

It is very curious how few generals there are in the world and how few leaders in religion.

Of course there are a lot about them but you do not hear about them, not we.

It is one of the things I always wonder when there are so many how comes it that there are so few. Just so few.

Grant was a general so they said and they knew and he was, he was married, he was a father, he was a general, he was a president, he was a traveler, he was a writer and a reader and he was dead. This is what they said.

Volume XI

HIRAM ULYSSES GRANT was a leader in religion. No one has said this, no, not any one, but it is true just as true as though everybody had said it who had heard it and now they read it.

Listen to it. Grant was a leader in religion.

Volume XII

How can there be so few of anything, generals and leaders of religion, just as if there is, and I do say it, no waiting and no preparing for it. Nobody waits to be a great man and so that is what it is.

There is no such thing as waiting. Let everybody know it, there is no such thing as waiting.

Volume XIII

HIRAM ULYSSES GRANT was not born. He was a leader in religion. He was not born because that is of no importance. Being born is of no importance, it is important only to fathers and mothers and grand-mothers and grandfathers and not even really to aunts and uncles; and so Hiram Ulysses Grant was not born.

Mr. Simpson was interested and not for nothing. He was so interested that if Grant was a general and had gone to West Point and everything he would have the name, and he was known as Ulysses Simpson Grant, and it does not make any difference.

Here we see where we are three if not two. One if not two.

No of course it makes no difference to a leader in religion, because a leader in religion can change his name. Saints change their name have changed their name always have changed their name. Of course they have had it. Even a general can change his name but he does not do it all the time. Not at all now.

Anybody can change their name and they do it too. But that is another question and can later express something as you will hear to see when I write about Wilbur Wright. Not that he did but some one else did, who was another Wilbur. But this is just to whet your appetite.

Grant was a leader in religion. Do you know which Grant. Which Grant is it. Which is the Grant that is the leader in religion and which is the Grant that is not. And have they had or ever had any connection. Have they or have they not. How many can answer.

Once more I ask you all not what is a leader in religion but what is religion. What is religion as American religion. I ask you all what it is what is religion what is it what is it as it is American religion.

The only way to know about religion is this, that they need not compare. There are no comparisons there. As I look at a great many sitting there there is no way to undertake to compare anything with anything. And so they are all longer there. They are all longer there than if in any way there was a way to compare anything with anything.

Do you wonder now do you wonder why I know what religion is.

Think think of a Grant, Hiram or General Grant, Hiram Ulysses or Lieutenant Grant, think of them. Do think of them.

What is religion. American religion.

Religion or and American religion.

Religion which is American religion.

Do I know what religion is.

I can answer that.

Religion is not leaving in anything, that is leaving it in, leaving in anything that has been left, as it was, just before they came to religion.

Think of Grant. Which Grant.

Did he leave in anything.

Think of Grant. He did not leave in anything.

It is not necessary to say which Grant. Do you see how it is not necessary.

No one can say that he was leaving anything in and why not. The answer is because he was not waiting. Of course that is the answer. You know now that that is what the answer is always is.

Waiting not being existing, leaving anything in is not being existing. Is there any difference between leaving anything in and leaving in anything. There is not.

And in this way a saint can change his name. Listen while I think again.

Grant and religion.

Religion and Grant.

Which Grant.

Not, and about this there is no doubt, not Ulysses Simpson Grant.

What is religion. Do you know what religion is. I do and so did Grant. I will not now say that I know which Grant but you do and I do, so we may and can say we do.

Grant did not say what religion is but I will. But he was a leader in religion. Hiram Ulysses Grant was a leader in religion. And I I will say what it is to be a leader in religion, and the way to say what is a leader is to say Hiram Ulysses Grant was such a one. One who was one. Who was a leader in religion in American religion. One.

There is no waiting in religion, there is no preparing in religion there is no leaving anything in, in religion. This is all that there is of religion of American religion.

There is nothing more nor is there anything more in American war. There is nothing more not there in American everywhere or anywhere. Which is which.

How can there be a difference between war and not war between religion and where. How can there be a difference between American and there between anywhere and everywhere between there and where. There is **none**.

The silence and the silence comes the silence is not there. This is because which is which and that is what they guess. See how funny it is with a Grant if he is a Grant there. See how much it is when it is that they like which they feel that their name is.

For them more for them than with them they need not have this. They could have any name which is a name. Is it all the same to have any name which is a name.

A name is a name if no one has it as a name, but when and if anybody has the same name is it still not only a name.

Think everybody think of their own name just like that.

Think of Hiram.

Just like that.

Think of Ulysses.

Just like that.

Sam just like that.

Do not think of Simpson just like that, that is not at all necessary.

There are not their only names. Lots of names are not their only names.

I never knew any one not to have a name. Did you. If they have a name then somebody can come with that name to make a name. So many change the names in which it is a name. This is so very known that nobody asks was it his name.

Did Hiram do so.

He did not.

Did Ulysses do so.

Ulysses was not his name.

Did Sam do so.

Sam was not his name.

Did Simpson do so.

Simpson was not his name.

What was his name.

Ulysses Simpson Grant was his name.

But then there is Hiram Ulysses Grant and they are not brothers. Therefore not everything that is religion is just as clear as which it is.

How can any one be a leader in religion. Just think. How can any

one be a leader in religion. But they can. Hiram Grant could and did.
He was a leader in religion. This is a feeling.

Volume XIV

WHEN no one asks for an answer, that means, that either everybody
knows or if they know they do not answer.

No one asks what is religion because, as no one asks, no one asks for
an answer.

It is just like that not only in religion but in America and in war. If
no one asks for an answer, no one asks because they do know and they
do not ask and they do not answer.

But they might ask if they know, or they might say they might
not ask if they could not answer, or they could know that they could
ask for an answer. In American it is just like that.

In American war it is just like that.

To be a leader in American religion where no one can be a leader that
is to say there can be a leader there can be leaders but there is no leading,
because there is no leading, they can all know the answer. They can ask
for the answer. This is the answer.

And do you know the difference between like and alike.

To ask for an answer is not an answer for American war for American
religion for America. No one asks.

Everybody asks and everybody can answer.

All of which is so strange if everybody is interested in me.

In American religion that is not so and that is why America is where
it is in war if in war, in religion always in religion in America as in
America.

That is to say there are leaders in religion in war in America but there
is no leading. Do you see. Yes you do see.

Religion may be made as Grant is made a leader in religion. You say
leader and no leading what is that. But that is just what America is,
just what it is, just that. And as many have us as ours are.

No one slowly thinks of General Grant. I do.

By the time I was stopped I knew when to stop. This was not true.
Not through Grant not to you.

Grant when he came too.

But no one is stopped no one is to stop not they, not in American war not in America not in American religion. They do do other things if they do but that has nothing to do with stop now has it.

Now it can be true that this makes me aware of why I stopped. I stopped when I came. And now I say. This is a Grant.

It is so easy to leave Grant to lose Grant to have Grant, any Grant it is so easy.

It is so easy always to know what Grant did or did not have to do. He did not have it to do. This was why he was a Grant.

He did not have it to do.

He was not there to be through.

But what was it when it was finished. When it was finished it was a war. But what had it been before. Before it had not been a war, it had been what they were doing as you know.

And what they had been doing. Yes. They did not all have to know what they were doing not of course. Of course they did which they did because they said what they did which is of course when they did what they did. And yet you all can know that Grant never said what is there to say which is to say that like that he said it. They said he did not say it. But he did. What was it he said. I want you to see just how to say it.

Did I ever hear of him before. And however often I speak of him do I have to begin over again. How did I first become acquainted with General Grant.

I first became acquainted with U. S. Grant. After that for a long time I was acquainted with General U. S. Grant. How did I become acquainted with General U. S. Grant. By reading about him of course by seeing his photograph often of course, by feeling that he was a great man often of course, and not feeling that General Lee was a great man at all. And now I have not changed my mind.

There have been a great many wars in the world and most of them were interesting. Wars are interesting. Are they more interesting than anything else. Perhaps yes. At any rate they are interesting. Why are wars interesting.

Wars are interesting, not because something is always happening, during a war not because of that, not because a war is showing every-body what had been happening before the war commenced. These are all reasons why wars are interesting but it is not the very real reason, why wars keep on going. It is the reason why wars are commencing but it is not the reason why wars are interesting. Wars are interesting because there is a back and forth every minute in a war and that is interesting.

Wars would not be interesting if there was not a back and forth but of course there is this in war and so wars are interesting.

There is more back and forth in war than there is even in dancing or in kissing and so war is interesting.

Forward and back and back and forth, and so wars are interesting.

In other things in anything in almost anything there is a back and forward forward and back but there are other things happening but in a war nothing is happening but that.

It is like dancing and therefore wars are interesting. Nobody can deny it.

To come back to war.

There are two reasons for war.

One reason is this. During peace there is something happening, any-thing is happening some are saying yes and some are saying no but a great many are not saying anything, of course not in peace. And so there is a forward and back but it is very slow in pushing very very slow. But it has pushed and one or a one has pushed the other one. Very well.

Having pushed or been pushed slowly been pushed or pushed those pushing or being pushed do not know but they a little know which has been pushing the other one from where he was before. They know the pushed and the pusher which one has pushed and they need no war to know it more. They can know it more but really, alright they know it. But then all those not the pushing those, not the pushed those, all those all those many those the ones in peace neither pushed nor pushing they do not know about who has won before there is a war. Of course they do not know but they have to know they have to be told so and the only way that they can know that they can be told so is by a war.

Now think about General Grant and the American war about the Mexican war about the Spanish war about the world war about any war. The pushed had been pushed off before the war and the pushed and the pusher really did not want the war, it is all who live around and have not heard of pushing or of being pushed who have to have the war. They want to see if that is so. Interesting if true. Show me I'm from Missouri, and so there is a war to show them but all the real pushing has been done before the war. The war just shows them. Sometimes in a war there is a surprise but not often. I say sometimes in the way a war comes out there is a surprise but I really do not believe it. It is not true. Of course there is no surprise. All the real pushing has been done already, every bit of it and then there is the war, but the pusher and the pushed they know who wins before there is the war. That is so. Nor is it so or is it not so. Well it is so.

Then they like the war and that is alright too.

Because as I said there is every minute in a war a forward and back and what is so nice as forward and back. Nothing, and that is why they all like it like they do.

Grant he never said war was hell or was anything new. No he just said I will fight it out on this line if it takes all summer, and he knew before he had begun that he was through of course he knew. And he knew before, he knew it as well before as he could know what he knew, and so he was not waiting. Do you see now why there is no waiting. Do you see. No waiting in war, no waiting in America no waiting in religion no waiting anywhere. Do you begin to see.

Now religion and war is not exactly the same now is it, even American religion and American war. Now is it.

Was Grant a leader in religion. I think so. Was he a general. I think so. Is war interesting. Yes I think so. Is religion interesting. Yes I think so. Is it interesting in the same way. No I do not think so. Were there two Grants. Yes I think so. Was one a leader in religion. Yes I think so. Was one a leader in war. Yes I think so. Were they both interesting. Yes I think so.

Which brings it back again to forward and back and the difference between war and religion, American war and American religion.

In other things than war and religion things are happening that have nothing to do with forward and back but in wars nothing is happening that has not to do with back and forward and forward and back, and that is the reason that wars are interesting. Anybody and everybody is interested in forward and back and back and forth and back and forward and this is something that is completely occupying the attention and everybody likes their attention to be completely occupied that is the way not to be lonesome and so that is the reason why war is interesting, there is no time wasted and so nobody is lonesome. Yes you do see. How can you waste time how can time be wasted when forward and back and back and forward is everything and it is always going on as it is a war.

Of course it is interesting, of course war is interesting.

In other things something or nothing is happening until there is no more to happen. Everybody likes that, it is their life just like that and it is interesting but not as occupying to the attention as forward and back and back and forward. It is not at all likely that it could be as interesting as naturally it does not hold the attention and so naturally it can be lonesome. Most naturally.

Peace has its victories as well as war. Sure. But it takes more time to go back and forward and forward and back in peace than in war and so most everybody stops looking. That is it. Most everybody stops looking.

And this brings me back to Grant.

Do you see why he is a leader in religion.

Because in war he knew so much about going forward and back and back and forward that to him it looked like waiting and as he knew that there is no such thing as waiting, that waiting is not existing; hear me say, he was a leader in religion Hiram Ulysses Grant was a leader in religion. Hiram Grant or Ulysses Grant, did he feel himself to be Hiram Grant. Nobody has ever said anything about this. And this is what I mean.

What is the difference between war and religion. You all know now what war is, American war, now what is religion, American religion.

What is American religion.

There there nobody can offer religion to him, to Hiram Grant. Can offer him religion.

In any case in no way can there be anything done which is not known and can be known as religion. Oh yes as religion.

I offer what I have to say.

What is religion. American religion.

About forward and back and religion, you know all about it now in war in any war now how about it in religion in any religion in American religion.

There is no forward and back in religion not even in camp-meeting it does not even look as if it is.

You see that.

There is no forward and back in American religion and therefore American religion is not like European religion. European religion is forward and back standing still, do you see what I mean but of course you do. American religion is not forward and back standing still, it is neither forward and back nor is it standing still. Think of a camp-meeting. Think also of what I have said about there being no sky in American religion, think also of what I said that it did not make any difference in a camp-meeting if the trees all were away to stay away it made no difference no difference at all.

There is no forward and back and staying quiet no standing still in American religion. It is like there being no sky it is there, as they know, there is no sky not that they ever think about the sky not even when they are killed and do not die, not they.

American religion is not only remarkable in not separating anything from anything or even in uniting. Nor even in untying. Nor in measuring. Nor in utilising.

In American religion they do not think of meadows and water. In American religion there is nothing of meadows having water in them and that to this water there is no name given. So she says. You see how it is not like European religion.

In American religion there is, so she says, but there is no having land and water nor water and land nor trees nor flowers nor sky nor changes, none of this has anything to do with American religion, and therefore American religion is not like European religion not at all not at all not at all.

Think how none of these things were interesting to Hiram Grant. He was not waiting to hear why it was not happening. He knew enough to say so but he never spoke. Why should one hear and speak. Whether he did hear was of no importance.

That is what makes American religion. Do you begin to see what makes American religion, what it is, what is American religion. It is why American religion is what it is. Yes it is.

I was with Grant.

Hiram Ulysses Grant was not forgotten. Why was he not forgotten. He was not forgotten because he was. He was not forgotten because they knew that they could say I was with Grant.

It is now forgotten that they could say, I was with Grant.

He is not forgotten because he was a leader in religion. Hiram Ulysses Grant. That is to say he is forgotten but I remember him.

Is there any change.

I ask you is there any change.

No there is not and I cannot ask you too often.

Does it make any difference

Does it mean anything.

Will you go away.

And if not why not.

And does it make any difference.

If it means anything does it make any difference and does it mean anything.

Will you go away.

And is Ulysses Simpson Grant real and was he born Hiram Ulysses. Oh yes he was, well not born, but certainly he was named Hiram Ulysses after he was born. He certainly was.

And if not why not, why was he born and named and afterwards his name was changed.

All of this that makes me say this makes me come to relieve everyone of this.

Do you understand.

I mean that I do not wish any one to be bothered by his having been named Hiram and not have been called Hiram. This might easily bother a great many.

Some can ask me do you understand. And I say yes I understand.

Of course if I understand I say that Hiram Ulysses Grant was born in some part of a day. Do you see how that makes of him a leader in religion. But not only that. Being born in some part of a day does make him a leader in religion. He was not only that being that. Does it make him a leader in American religion or not. Do you see how it is just doubtful. A little bit doubtful that it does make him a leader in American religion, just that. Perhaps it does not make him just that, just that does not just make him that, a leader in American religion perhaps not just that.

He was born in some part of a day, that is he was born and then he was named Hiram Ulysses he was named that on a day.

Did this make him a leader in religion. Is that what they say. It could make him a leader in religion but not a leader in American religion, no not any such thing. Do you begin to understand, yes or no.

There is no use in now saying, if he had been a leader in religion.

Can you see how this can make him a leader in religion in one way. Oh yes you can see.

There is no use in now saying that he had been a leader in religion in American religion. The thing now to say is how can he and not any one be a leader in religion. That is the thing to say now.

The rest of it I can say anyhow.

A leader in religion, because how does he become a leader in religion if now he is a leader in religion.

He is so well-known now.

He is well known now by having his name well-known well-known now.

Ulysses Simpson Grant a leader in religion. That is a question.

Hiram Ulysses Grant a leader in religion, yes a leader in religion.

How well I remember that they are all killed and so they do not die like they do in Europe, not they. They are killed every day and that was always so, just so and is yet even yet so, oh yes it is so, it is even yet so as you know.

And this has nothing to do with war American war nothing at all but it has to do with American religion which it is. Of course it is. It also has to do with there being no leading in American religion. It has also to do with a Grant being a leader in religion and all this has to be said until not any one can be dead not any one.

I mean just this.

I have just said that there is no such thing as a leader because as they are all there they cannot despair. This makes American religion, really and truly it does.

They can be afraid and care, they can be religious and dare, but they cannot compare and as they cannot compare, there is no way to compare one thing with another thing there, there are no leaders there. Oh how can you cry because you cannot try.

Have you forgotten what Hiram looked like and what he was because I have not. I could not forget because it is his name. Hiram Ulysses Grant. Do you remember what his name looked like and what he looked like. Of course you really do.

All this makes no humility.

Let me think about all the things that are not in religion in American religion. Their name and why they came and where they were and how they looked and what they said and when they were dead. None of these things have anything to do with American religion no they have not. There there it is American religion is not where it is, not there, but it is oh yes it is not even enough. There is no enough and no sky in American religion and no try. Now it sounds like that but is it, no it is not.

I like American religion and they have it. Remember there is no day and night of course not of course there is not. Do you see how just it is not like European religion do you see, it sounds like nothing but it is it is American religion yes it is.

Humility, changes, reprisals, absences, waiting, allowance, restraint, advantage, organisation, reliance, facility, separation, reparation, absence, division and subtraction. All these things are not in religion in American religion, not, they are not.

And names. Who names names. Nobody names names. They have names. If they have names and nobody names names, names are not like names, but they will know their names. Oh yes their names. It is like that their names.

What then is there in religion in American religion.

There is no waiting in religion in American religion.

I have just been reading that there is no waiting in American religion.

What is there in American religion.

There is no leading in American religion.

If not why not, oh yes you know you all know there is no leading in American religion.

What then is there in American religion.

There is no advice in American religion. If there is no advice and you know of course you know that there is no advice in American religion then of course then there is no advice in American religion.

Now when you think of all this you will see why Hiram Ulysses Grant was a leader in religion in American religion just like that.

What is in religion. He is in religion. He Hiram Ulysses Grant. He is not outside in religion. Nor does he mean to kneel. Nobody knows that in American religion, not they. They stood, standing is standing. They are standing holding something or just standing, in American, in American religion, now they are sitting just sitting, in American, in American religion. That is the only difference between then and now. In American in American religion. Yes of course you know that if you think of that. Remember how they stood then how they sit now, but that is alright, then they stood because they stood and rode now they sit because they sit and ride. Yes you do see that all of you do see that.

Let me tell a little story. Once when Hiram Ulysses Simpson Grant was sent to buy a pony, his father said, offer the man twenty dollars and if he will not take it offer him twenty-two and if he will not take it offer him twenty-four and if he will not take it do not offer him any more.

But he will take it. The man was told the story of what his father said
by Hiram Ulysses Simpson Grant and he did take it.

Let me tell another story.

Once when Grant was careful to be where he was Ulysses Simpson
Grant he was, some one asked him did he come there to wait for anything. No one heard the answer.

And a great many people knew that he had come when he did and
that no one heard the answer.

Do you see how there is no kneeling in America, in American
religion, not like that no waiting and no kneeling, no not like that.

There is no doubt in any one's mind that Grant was not waiting. Oh
no not that.

Hear me while I tell what they know.

Volume XV

OH yes I know what they know and this makes religion.

Every now and then Grant listened when they told that there were
other men who had come, not to find him, but to know where he was.

Volume XVI

AND this makes religion. Hiram Grant. Yes or no. Hiram Ulysses Simpson Grant. Oh how do you know.

He never said I like, out loud.

He never said that they might be wakeful. He never said he knew
what was a philopena or a valentine. Of course he did know and that
made anybody anxious. He was a leader in religion.

In his time there were philopenas and valentines.

Philopinas are when there are two kernels in a nut and when they
are first seen they are seen and they said philopena. Anybody can know
that just as he did he did know that.

A valentine is different. There can be kinds of valentines. There can
be comic valentines and sweet valentines and funny valentines. Of
course he could know that he did know that, he had that he had it to
have to know that which of course he did. He knew all of that.

There is a short history of a man.

It is very nice.

It is this.

He was a soldier at fifteen, he was a general at twenty-three, and he was dead on the field of battle at twenty-seven. Then there was a monument to him in the public square of the city in which he was born made within two years of when he was no more.

Contrast a career like this with that of General Grant General Ulysses Simpson Grant.

Grant was not like that but anybody can know that. A man like that would not know what a philopena was what a valentine was. But Grant did. He knew.

Think how they know and how they like a philopena and a valentine.

They know, they know that a philopena is when there are two nuts in one kernel and that is just the way they grew and they knew just what there was to do when they found the two nuts in the kernel where there might only be one. They knew just what to do. Of course he knew, even if he did not do what there was to do. Yes of course he knew.

A valentine is St. Valentine's day in February and they can send each other paper that looks like lace or comic valentines.

What part had these things in Grant's life. He certainly could like them both.

Before Grant knew he was going to change his name he knew about valentines. Did anybody ever send any one by the name of Hiram a valentine. He did not wonder why not. They did send one by the name of Ulysses a valentine, and valentines are very welcome when they come, and philopenas are very welcome when they are found.

Nobody thinks of this in connection with Ulysses S. Grant but why not. You have to think of it when you think of what Grant would have been if he had been a leader in religion, and he was, he was a leader in religion.

If any one had sent him a valentine it would not have been a lace one it would not have been a comic one it would have been a nice one. And perhaps only two were sent to him. I do not think that there were many sent to him or one or none. I think two were sent to him. Two were sent to him. Each one of them was a nice one.

He did not often find philopenas in nuts and yet it did not surprise him when he did find them although it was exciting for him. It was not exciting to him to find them but it excited him. In this way you could know that he could come to be a leader in religion.

What is religion.

Religion is not a surprise, but it is exciting.

War is a surprise and is not exciting sometimes not. Think of Grant, in a way war was a surprise he knew about war about any war but just as a war is not a war and it is not a war because there was not to be this war just for all those reasons war is a surprise but not exciting. Religion is not a surprise but it is exciting. You begin to see that. Grant was not there to be relieved by a surprise he never had been. He never had been relieved by any surprise.

Some people can be relieved by a surprise and they can make a war but not Ulysses Simpson Grant he could not be relieved by a surprise and so to him war was not exciting. You do, but yes you do, you do understand.

To be a leader in religion in American religion there is no leading in American religion, Grant Hiram Ulysses Grant could receive did receive when he was receiving did receive not a great many valentines, but only two, and those not comic, nor lace ones, but very nice ones.

That is one side of religion and Grant had this in him.

What happened now to him to make him a leader in religion.

But first I did not raise my boy to be a soldier but any of them are and why not when every one of them are. Why not. If not. Why not. But they are. Being a soldier comes naturally to any one. They say no they say yes but there you are it does come naturally to any one.

War does not come so naturally but being a soldier yes of course yes.

Religion does religion come naturally to any one not so naturally as being a soldier not quite so natural. They do not say yes and they do not say no quite no naturally about religion and they do not do so so naturally they do not. Not about religion. And yet religion is not an unnatural thing not at all it is not as natural a thing as being a soldier because after all it is not just acting it is something that has to be remembered and separated and that is a thing that has more distance than just being a soldier. I do not say that war is more natural than religion but being a soldier is more natural than religion yes a little more natural. Do you not think so.

Even American religion which is very natural it is natural to an American to have American religion he has to in a way remember or separate something but being a soldier is more natural, nobody not anybody has to remember or separate anything to be a soldier. To be a soldier is just that. They all or any of them are just that.

A good many think that it is not only not why they go but why they are as they are, that makes of them a soldier.

Remember the one who was a soldier at fifteen a general at twenty-three and dead of wounds at twenty-seven and a column erected to him before two years were over. Grant was not like that. Nobody who went to West Point was like that. In the first place they could not be because it was there that they were quiet and not waiting, and it was there that they were staying while they were left alone.

As I say it is natural for them not to be like that at West Point but to be soldiers, any of them.

I remember this in this late war which was just like the Civil war only more so. By this I mean just this. Anybody could be a soldier which is not what makes a war. Not at all what makes a war. Anybody can be soldiers, that is just this. I did not raise my boy to be a soldier. No of course not but if not why not since at any rate that has nothing to do with this that anybody is a soldier as I say. Of course anybody can say yes to this of course they can if they will, of course they will not if they can not but it is true just as they say oh yes we do.

Alright I remember how there were french soldiers and American soldiers any of them were natural soldiers. And then there was the fourth of July and then there was the fourteenth of July. Anybody can be natural soldiers on the fourth of July as well as on the fourteenth of July just like that. Alright just like that.

On the fourth of July the Americans marched first and then the french. The Americans marched well, their step and they looked like that, solemn like that, they marched like that, all was well. The french marched but not like that they were natural soldiers just like that, but not like that, just as well, because they were beginning, just as well, to commence, just as well, to become, just as well, the kind of soldiers they were to become which was war. That is what is war do you see what is war. Perhaps you do. I do very plainly and I hope you do. If not you will. Of course you will, if not what will you do. But of course you will.

The next day which was fourteenth of July. The french led, they marched very well they marched as soldiers march who will or will have to march, march they will, war they will, why not war if they will, of course if they will. This they do not only they will but they do. The Americans marched after and they did not march so well. I cannot say that they did march so well. Of course they did not not on the fourteenth of July. They did on the fourth of July. Do you understand, everybody everybody everybody do you understand.

Volume XVII

It is funny that long ago soldiers were members of religion and members of religion were soldiers just like that. And now and then, even then when Grant was at West Point they were not members of religion if you like, that is they had it as they had, had religion, but it was not as a soldier or as a member of religion that they had all they had. If they had it they had it but not as an order not in order to be a soldier. They were not soldiers if you like, but they were quiet. They always are at West Point. That is what makes them different from any other school, this that they are quiet. In a way it never leaves them, not as quiet, but as having been, not quiet, but where they were as it is quiet. I like this about West Point. Grant did. Not that he liked it but he did. He knew the difference between quiet and waiting and he knew there is not any such thing as waiting.

There is of course no such thing as waiting.

Thank you for all your kindness, was never said by Grant.

It is very hard to remember how often he got up and how often he went to bed.

It is very hard to remember how often he went to bed and how often he got up at West Point and how often he got up and how often he went to bed after West Point.

At any rate at West Point they called him Sam Grant. This meant very much or something to them. It may have meant something, but it most likely did not mean anything to him. It certainly meant nothing to any one who only saw, heard or knew about him.

And so I think one might almost leave the name Sam out. Nothing should be left out that has once been in.

If you left anything out that has once been in you do do that thing. That is the way to make a thing not mistaken but not really interesting. By leaving anything out that has once been in, you make it not really interesting, not really.

I said there where they were at school at West Point they were quiet. In a way that is the way they are when religion and war is one, that is one and one which makes it one.

That is the way they were long ago when religion was fighting and fighting was religion, war nobody said, war. They may be soldiers but there may not be war neither now nor by and by.

But listen.

In America then is was and has been fighting and religion. Remember everything of course it has been that soldiers and religion made them do their fighting being the kind who gave and had orders given or acted without as many Americans do.

They do act without orders they act with orders they like orders, or if not they do as they do. This is what they are.

Remember I always said leaders in religion, yes leaders in religion but is there leading. No there is no leading there are leaders in religion but there is no leading that is in American religion in American anything. Yes I know this is true and so do you. Oh yes so do you. Of course yes so do you.

It is queerly there that they do not care, not at all but they need to they need that orders are orders and leading is not leading. Do you see the difference and see how that makes America. Yes you do. Most certainly yes you do. I do so most most certainly you do.

Think about how they bought and how they fought, how they fight and how they buy. Of course just this and you will see what I say, there are ordering and orders there are leaders but no leading, none at all none none at all.

Remember when there was religion and soldiers it was true too it always is true. There are leaders in religion but no leading and Hiram Ulysses Grant was a leader in religion and Ulysses Simpson Grant was a leader in war but there is in war or will be no leading no no leading. Just like that no leading.

Grant went to school. He came nearly every day to school but nobody thought of him then as Grant. Naturally they would not. Nobody thought of him as a leader in religion. Nobody thought of him as a general no certainly not as a lieutenant general.

At that time he was at school almost every day, which is the way to go to school. When you are at school everybody who is at school knows you are at school, only they may forget about it. They can forget just as easily if you are going to be a leader in religion, a lieutenant general, or nothing at all.

It is easy to forget and it is easy not to forget who went to school with you with whom you went to school, who was at school when you were at school.

What did one do at school, what does one do at school.

After all nothing is changed, one does something when one is at school.

That is what I always say nothing is changed. They say everything is changed but is it. No it is not changed because I could have gone to school with any of them. That shows that nothing has changed, the way you could go to school with any one you went to school with and no matter how long ago you went to school or how just now they went to school you could have gone to school with been at school come to school in and out of school with them. That is the way you know it has not changed no matter how much they say it has. You could have gone to school with any of them. And they could do what they do or did do. They went to school and you could or have gone to school with any of them. So of course it has not changed. It is just like that always yet and still.

But that makes it sure that it is very strange how few there are of how few it is true, shame shame fie for shame everybody knows your name, or just the same without the shame everybody knows your name. And how does it happen and has it anything to do with whom you went to school. I wonder.

Anyway one thing is sure, really sure that when you are in school everybody knows your name. Of course they do anybody who is there is just the same. Everybody knows your name. Later on it is not so true it surely is not so true that everybody knows your name. There are just those a few, and of those few although they went to school too, everybody knows your name. Yes this is fame.

These things have nothing to do with anything, as for instance, any one can remember.

I want gradually to know just how few who have been to school and then everybody knew everybody's name came later to have it be the same that everybody knows your name. And did anybody know it then know it really truly certainly and surely of them, the ones who are the few, would anybody know, is it true, that anybody knows it then, even those who are the ones to be the ones, shame shame fie for shame everybody knows your name. Or anyway in any way everybody knows your name.

By this I mean just this did anybody really truly know it of you that you would be one of the few that everybody would know of you, that everybody would know your name.

It is very funny the things that make this true. And do I know it or do you. I wonder. I wonder if I will know why, even when how hard I try, and I wonder too whether if I ever do know, why no matter how hard I try, I can make you know why, if there is a why to know. I do wonder. I do wonder so very much. Yes I do.

I do wonder so very much if there is a why to know. Does anybody know why they are there and everybody knows your name without any shame shame fie for shame. Does anybody really know the reason why and was anybody really and truly sure, really and truly sure when you went to school. I wonder and I wonder why. Now I will try to tell why.

What is the reason and how many are there but gradually we will that is I will come back to that.

Almost everybody when they go to school goes to school almost every day. Grant did this. He was not Grant then. He was something else then. It would be as well to know what.

But to me it makes no difference as I never knew any one called Hiram or any one called Ulysses. I did not know anybody called Hiram or Ulysses when I was at school I did not know anybody called Hiram or Ulysses later.

Hiram Ulysses Grant. That is different. Ulysses Simpson Grant, that is different too. Knowing it just like that is different too.

Volume XVIII

THE thing always worries me is how you whose name everybody knows is different from those whose name nobody knows. You nor I nor nobody knows where peas and beans and barley grows. And of course nobody knows. Did Ulysses Simpson Grant know, he only knew as I know as he knows as anybody knows. Did he know when he was at school. Just as they all knew when they were at school. And who knew who was who. Nobody did know. No nobody knew or knows.

But they do go to school. You naturally anybody can will or shall go to school, have been at school. And therefore America is just the same. That is what I say. You could always have gone to school with any of them. Of course. That never is any different, you could you can you will always have been likely to go to school with any of them. Oh yes. When you see them or have seen them or do see them. Yes.

What happened next to Ulysses S. Grant. After he went to school while he went to school he changed his name. Did he change it himself or did they change it and did he like or did he mind it. It does make a difference of course. If you have one name and you know what it is and you have another name and you get to know what it is it does make a difference, of course. Then he went to West Point and there he had another name, they called him Sam and that made a difference only it does not seem to have made a difference, not really made a difference.

And then he had a title and that was another change of name. He was Lieutenant Ulysses Simpson Grant and then that made that difference it could make a difference but did it. It began by making a difference. Well anything can make a difference and that made a difference.

And then pretty soon he did not have a title any more and he was Grant and there it was, it again made a difference, it made just that difference. Nobody neglected that.

But never forget Hiram Ulysses Grant who is a leader in religion. He had no changes in his name, not any change not any time in his name and that made no difference, because he had been used to it, used to not, to it not making any difference all the same.

It is very easy to love one of two. There was a moment there were three. There were Hiram Ulysses Grant, Hiram Grant, Ulysses Simpson Grant and then there were two. After there were two then there was almost one and there was a loss. They felt they fell away and they did and nobody remembered or forgot, them.

Even I never remembered or forgot one of them.

Come again.

Hiram Ulysses Grant. Do not forget it is Hiram Ulysses Grant not Ulysses S. Grant. He was one who did never come back suddenly. It was not as a photograph that he was there, he had to be remembered by how he came to be there, there where he always was. His beard his drink his eyes his tallness and his ways and what he said. Only he did not say that he would say anything to be alone with him. He could be worn out too, any one could if the weather was right to wear any one out, of course which they did. Which was if it did.

Do you begin to see. I wish you would.

Any weather is the same when it is all where it is and he would not say what it was. He could know of course he could know very well what the weather was but that made no exchanges in religion. No exchange in anything. There was enough of it to be, which it always is as they like. No need to like it. There is the difference between like and alike. This is the difference. They need no help at all. Not he.

Do you begin to see.

Do you begin to see that if the weather is there, wear me out, but not worn out not by any weather whether or not whether. You do you begin to see as well as know which is why it is that I do not have to tell you so. No.

Was he a leader in religion. He almost forgot that.

Anybody could almost forget what, what he was.

Just as they like. Much as they like.

Do not be careful to be alone. Nobody in America need be careful to be alone, not in American religion not to be careful to be alone.

Do you understand what that means Lizzie do you understand. Do you understand about alone and nobody in America need be careful to be alone. I guess yes you understand. Oh yes.

Do you see once again how different American religion is from European religion. Just in one thing like that.

No one in American religion needs to be careful to be alone.

I can see Ulysses Simpson young, I can see him being young.

I cannot see Hiram Ulysses young but I must or it is all wrong. If he is not young, has been, he is not a leader in religion but he is, he is a leader in religion, and now I see his photograph when he was young, when Hiram Ulysses Grant was young. Did he have a photograph taken then, it does not make any difference Hiram Ulysses Grant was young. I know how he looked in his photograph even if there was none taken of him when he was young. That was a mere accident of how it happened.

Volume XIX

Now you know there are two and one is connected with American religion and one is connected with American war.

They are there and they are now connected with everywhere.

Everything is now where there is that there is American religion and American war.

By this I mean that American religion and American war is like re-

ligion and like war everywhere. What I mean is that they all have come
to that. You all, they all. We came first.

Not to remember war.

Not to remember any war American war or any war.

But to remember American religion more and more. Let us.

What is the use of remembering war because anybody will remember
it as much more, they will remember what a war was before and after
and because it was and Grant was Ulysses Grant was U. S. Grant was
before and after and there was that war but there is no use in remembering any war. I have made that clear. War is forward and back and interesting but there is no use in remembering it. Not now anyhow.

Anybody can remember that, that war. Therefore there is not any
use in remembering war.

Grant knows that, if he knows when he was forward and back and
he knew that, it was not exciting, not even to him it was not even
interesting that a war was as well as has been, is as well as was will be or
has been.

He did not talk about it like that. He knew when they went where
they went and as they went anyway what was the use of anything that
was not they.

That is what has happened now and now it will change, but enough
said.

What I wish to explain I will explain clearly.

Volume XX

I WILL finish with saying the daughter of Ulysses S. Grant married
into Europe. What does that do. That does not do anything.

Volume XXI

BUT before I finish I wish I will wish to say that to-day, to-day is like
that, to-day is the day when anybody can remember when anybody can
forget either Grant. They can remember and they can forget Hiram
Ulysses Grant. They can remember and they can forget Ulysses Simpson Grant. And anybody can almost cry not if they try to remember
or forget but just as it is as they feel. They feel like that to-day. They feel

that it can make them cry to forget Hiram Ulysses Grant or Ulysses Simpson Grant and they feel that it can make them cry to remember Hiram Ulysses Grant or Ulysses Simpson Grant.

And why is that.

This is what I wish to explain.

Hiram Ulysses Grant was one who was not there but there were just as many who were there who were like that, who were like him and he was like that. He was like that and he was a leader in religion like that only like that there was no leading in religion, there were camp-meetings in religion, he went there that is he was there but he never led a camp-meeting. He was not a leader in religion like that and indeed like that they did not lead in religion. If they led in religion they did not do anything. They neither fought nor bought not they although there was religion. In America there always is religion and just the same there always is religion.

Are we. That is not the question, but it is the answer in American religion.

You are coming back on Friday. Are we. That is the answer.

Do you see that or do you begin to see that.

Do you also begin to see that which makes me see how there is no use in any difference between any time in the life of Hiram Ulysses Grant. And why. Because as he was he was always as he was if he could and he did say are we, when there is no answer and no question asked as it is. It is not a question it is an answer. Are we, is an answer and an American answer and a religious answer and an American religious answer. Any American can see that when they say that, when he says that, when I say that. Are we. Of course they can and so they can and this makes it as it is. An American can. Are we. When he is told that he will be back on Friday.

Not yet has this American religion this which is an answer.

Are we, is an answer.

Yes it is, it is it was, it was it will it will be.

Religion will be.

American religion will be.

Oh yes it is.

Could America American religion change and if it did change could any one ask it why. I I do not believe so. I do not believe that it will be so. And of course. I do not believe that it will indeed that it will be so. And the reason why is this. If American religion could change then there would not be of course any other reason why.

But American religion cannot die nor do they die. And why. If they were killed they did not lie and die. They did not die. And why. In American religion they do not die, and if they shall not die. Why. Because why. But you all know that. If not now then when. But you do. Oh yes you do. You do know when and then as well as can not die.

What is American religion.

American religion is what they could not compare with themselves.

Forget or try to forget Hiram Ulysses Grant, which has been done.

Forget or try to forget Ulysses Simpson Grant and why has this been done.

This could be done if American religion had not come. But it has come and now even now they would forget just as other people like more than they like. But do other people like more than they like. Not any American can. No American can like more than they like, and this makes American religion, which if it can cannot like more than it can like. Do you see.

And so you see there is nothing European about that nothing at all European about that, that American religion can not like more than it can like.

So now do you begin to see why like and alike are not alike. But of course you do. Very well you do.

It would be sad to be glad that there was no American religion there anywhere. So sad to be glad about that that nobody did nobody was glad about that. If not sad it would be better that it did not happen to be there that there was no American religion anywhere.

American religion is just like that it can never make anybody go anywhere and there right there it is not like any European religion. Do you see that.

If everybody knew just how true it was that American religion is like that and everybody does know that American religion is like that then everybody can know that being there or not being there is not where there is anything to compare. In American religion there is nothing to compare.

Sometimes Hiram Ulysses Grant is so far away but American religion is not it is not far away, such a thing is not American religion, no not at all.

But sometimes Hiram Ulysses Grant is so far away. In the beginning he was not far away he was there but now is he there or is he only far away. Yes he is only far away. I can only say that yes he is only far away.

Ulysses Simpson Grant is as far away. He too is far away just as far away. American war is just as far away, as far away as he is as Ulysses Simpson Grant is, just as far away.

American religion is not far away not at all nor in any way far away. Just not that. American religion is not at all that. It is not that.

It never is that it never was that, is that or was that.

American religion is never far away. We know this is so. I say what you say and you say what I say. This is so.

And so does anybody really know what it matters if it is so that anybody who was so is far away. No it does not matter any more because American religion is there yes it is it is there. And it makes that difference to any one.

It is all over everywhere American religion is, not over or all over, but really everywhere. Now. Not over there, but there and everywhere, American religion is.

Any one who has no right and left no up and down no lend a hand knows what it is, they know that and now nobody should start. Why not. Because it is true American religion and American way to be and not to be away, that is to say the way American religion can be what they say, when they can come any day, to hear every day, to read any day, everything that they can carry away and all of them say. Like that.

I cannot tell you how often like and alike are not alike. This I cannot tell you how often.

What is American religion.

They all listen to that.

Listen, is just the same as listen to that.

Now how often have I said I never will know why Hiram Ulysses
Simpson Grant did not say so. No I never will know.

They often say. Say. Listen. Interesting if true.

Volume XXII

I CANNOT help thinking that I can make any of you understand that
American religion has spread. Yes it has. In Europe they think nothing
is there and that is because the sky is there but in America they know
it is there because there is no sky there.

Now yes you do understand.

Of course you do understand when I say it like that.

Any of you of course all of you which is of course any of you, all of
you can understand when I say it like that. Which I do when I do say
it like that. Which of course I do.

By this I mean, that the European sky can still lie over all like a sky
but the European knows about the American sky not being a sky like
that. Oh yes they do. They may say no but oh yes they do. This makes
them know what the American can and do do and they do it too. Oh
yes they do.

Now how can you account for Hiram Grant being a leader in religion
when there is no leading in American religion. But of course you do
account for it because there have been other ones and they were not at
all like that, not the least bit like that, not even different from being
like that not in any way like that nor different.

I have almost forgotten any and every Grant have you. But I have
not forgotten American religion nor have you, no not any of you, nor
have I forgotten what there is to do to finish for you too. What is there
to do if you have forgotten Hiram Grant and Ulysses Grant. Is there
anything to do. A great many have forgotten Hiram Grant and Ulysses
Simpson Grant. I had not but perhaps I have now. Perhaps I have. I
cannot say that it is not true that perhaps I have.

I remember Hiram Ulysses Grant. I have just remembered who he
was and what he did and when he came and what he looked like and
what they said when they saw him. But they did not say anything of
course not then not as much as they would like him to do. But he did

not do any'hing. No not then. Not then or ever after or before. Because nobody needed it. In American religion nobody needed it. Do you see why American religion is not European religion. Do you see. Or do you only begin to see. Which do you do.

In American religion nobody needed it.

Ulysses Simpson Grant. I can remember him.

I can remember him when he was dead that is to say I can remember him.

Volume XXIII

THEN they went to Europe oh yes they did he did.

Going to Europe was alright.

I always remember a story that pleased me about him. He had gone to see a house where the Duke of Wellington had been. How many men had he commanded at Waterloo he asked and he asked it because he wanted to say that. He did not say it because he wanted to do that. He did not say it because speaking of battles made him think of such a thing. The Duke of Wellington's son lied to him, he thought Ulysses S. Grant wanted to boast about commanding men.

Do you see why Europeans are as they are, naturally not, nobody can see why anybody is as they are.

It is a nice story and I always liked it like that.

This is a natural thing that nobody can see why anybody is as they are.

Ulysses Simpson Grant was then when he was an older man he was then a man who could ask that thing. Why not. If not then why not. That is everything.

That is one of the strangest things that then he was an American but does it make any difference if he is an American.

He had a daughter I said so and she married as a European.

And who could remember Hiram Ulysses Grant. Nobody or anything.

See the way I see this.   .

It comes as a shock Hiram Ulysses and everybody who had could forget him. Which was as alike.

When I came down not late in the evening but still in the evening to say something I said Grant was an American. I said this thing. I said it. I cannot deny but that I said it. I did say it. Grant was an American. Was he when he visited the Duke of Wellington. Was he when his daughter was married to a European. Was he or was he not or was he. Who can say what he was what he was then.

Do you see what I mean. Who can say what he was then.

This is Ulysses Simpson Grant of course. Yes of course.

Hiram Ulysses Grant would never have visited the Duke of Wellington he would never have had his daughter married to a European. Not he. And why not he. Because he was a tall thin man and he was drunk a little always often and standing and he was leading in religion in American religion, and he was not one any Duke of Wellington would have been writing to visit him because the Duke of Wellington would not have heard of him. Certainly not not any Duke of Wellington. Was he an American, not as American as Ulysses Simpson Grant had been. No not as American. He was not a failure in everything as Ulysses Simpson Grant had been which is something of course, it is something to be an American and to be failing in everything, not waiting, not failing because there is no such thing as American waiting and so there is no such thing as American failing, it sounds like not the same but it is. There is no such thing as American leading. No certainly not no certainly of course not. Why not. Because of course not.

Hiram Ulysses Grant is not forgotten that does not mean anything because nobody knows about him so anybody can remember him or remember about him.

Ulysses Simpson Grant can he be forgotten, can some and many in New York not know anything about who the Grant is of the Grant Memorial. And yes that is true and if it is so true how is it true. And now I will tell you.

I will tell you all there is about American.

Volume XXIV

I CANNOT forget everything I remember nor can they.

Volume XXV

I WHICH I have.

I can remember everything and I remember which I have not done not only now but always.

What was Grant when he was alive.

Can you remember the difference between he was alive and dying.

Can you remember the difference between he was dying and he was alive.

Of course you do. You can all remember his reminiscences too. Yes yes of course you do that is some of you do, perhaps yes with of course yes some of you yes some of you yes do.

What did Grant do.

Who knows what Grant did. I do.

This is natural because I know it too yes just as much as yes you do which you do Which of course you do.

Ulysses Simpson Grant do you remember the whole of it too.

My gracious yes you do.

Ulysses Simpson Grant was born Hiram Ulysses Grant. If I had not been careful to remember this it would have made all the difference and it still does. Oh yes it still does.

Hiram Ulysses Grant oh yes it still does.

Right right, right and left, left left, left right left. This does not make any difference much difference either.

Not only now but then not even then but then that is what they did then just as they did then. They did not die then or were killed then. Not they. Think then what they do now.

Oh yes you think you are very funny but think now what they did do then.

And think now.

I think now.

Yes I think I think now.

I think that Ulysses Simpson Grant is not the same as Hiram Ulysses Grant. I think that now.

I think that now although I lost it and now it was not to find it but to have it.

Now do you see you can love that is you can love having it, but you do not find it, not unless you have it.

You lost it.

You have it.

You did not find it.

See what I mean.

Ulysses Simpson was and is like that.

He is like that.

Hiram Ulysses Grant, he is not like that which is what I mean.

The more you know the more you see why Ulysses Simpson is the way I see, oh yes this way this is the way I see.

One two three all out but she.

Ulysses Simpson is the way I see.

Hiram Ulysses not at all.

And now do you see why he is tall.

If he is tall he is not at all not at all Ulysses Simpson Grant.

Of course you see.

Of course you do.

And if you do do you like what you do.

Yes you do.

Volume XXVI

I THINK I see why I am an American.

Ulysses Simpson Grant.

Hiram Ulysses Grant.

They are not the same.

Were they always so. Yes or no.

Volume XXVII

Now to steadily talk not to steadily walk or stand not to steadily see or say but may, may we do anything we know while we have it so. May we.

Ulysses Simpson Grant as I remember him, changes or not but he does not.

He never changes. No not for me. Not for his photograph.

Hiram Ulysses Grant does not but that is less interesting.

It is Ulysses Simpson Grant that is interesting very interesting.

Do you begin to see why he is interesting.

Just that do you begin to see why he is interesting.

If to be interesting is to be American and American religion is is American is it interesting. If to be interesting is American and if it is interesting if it is American then it is interesting, American religion is interesting and the reason why is this.

The reason why is that everything has been and has been coming, has come, and is after it has been that is has come, it is in its being, interesting it is being American religion which is interesting.

Just like that.

By that it is all this.

American religion has a way of making it be that hereafter it has been distributed everywhere just like that. Remember American religion is a religion where the sky is not there where you see when you look air is there but not the sky, and why because there is no sky no sky makes no heaven and a heaven makes a sky and that is why that now American religion is everywhere. Do you see that.

Because now everybody knows about heaven oh yes just yes everybody knows.

Little by little do you see that.

American religion did see that little by little and more and more American religion is there everywhere and just like that. It is clearly just like that, clear, that in any way, anything they say, they do not see but hear, and know and anybody can tell you so. Oh yes. Of course. Anybody can and anybody does and anybody was and they tell them so. There is no no they tell them so.

Yes that is American religion they tell them so. There is no not in American religion.

This which you see is all to me.

In any other religion they say no. In no American religion do they tell you no. No oh no.

And so how can they know that anything any one can tell them so does tell them so is told so.

Oh yes of course.

Everybody says, tell him so, and so everybody is as it is to do, to tell them so and not no.

By this I mean just this.

Once upon a time there was a place and this place was all full of space oh yes it was.

There was space above below right and left and no one left to tell any one so. Oh yes you know. You know that.

Then gradually then it was very well then that it made no difference then when. When anybody came and went, left or came or sat or stood or made or could be left alone. There was no such thing as being left alone. Not for any one. And so American religion was made. Do you see why it is different from European religion. In European religion you can be left alone but not in American religion. You do see that. Can you not see that.

And then so it can be that it made no difference and nobody ran. They may run for president that is a way to say but actually really and truly nobody ran nobody can. Do you see why I say that in American religion every day there are leaders to be sure but no leading. You see that do you not. Oh yes you do see that.

You see that now.

And so Hiram Ulysses he never ran he never sat he stood as he can, he can stand, most certainly he does he did and can but he never ran oh no he never could run. And why should anybody run when there is always the sun and anything else just as they can. Not that the sun makes any difference nor any weather which is to be had. It makes no difference not at all and any way.

Ulysses Simpson Grant was like that and he was not like that nothing could make any difference to him like that.

He did not know about to run. Do you see.

Volume XXVIII

ULYSSES SIMPSON GRANT was one who was not like that. He did not run he did not stand he did not move to stand or sit or run. He was one who did sit, any photograph can show that he sat, he never stood he did not stand he did not change to move he did not move to stand. He sat. Ulysses Simpson Grant sat.

Now think about two kinds of American religion, a religion where they stand and a religion where they sit but they do not sit and stand. No they do not stand and sit.

One is one and the other is one but neither one is two. That makes it sure that it is American religion which it is. American is American and American religion is American religion, it is like which it is.

Now just think of all American before you and you will see what I mean. Of course you will of course you will see what I mean.

Think of the whole American land and think of how they sit and think of how they stand and one does not do the two. No.

That is what I mean by American religion. Now Lizzie do you understand.

Volume XXIX

You do see how they stand and it is American religion.

You do see how they sit and it is American religion.

They stand and they sit and so they do not die but they do not do the two things not now not even by and by. Oh no.

You can be killed and you stand you can be killed and you sit but you do not die and why, because any American can, that is just what he does. If you can be killed you are not killed to die. Not now if not by and by. Do you see that.

And so you see that American religion is not European religion. Hiram Ulysses Grant, well that is not necessary now not if nobody wants to know why I think so.

But Ulysses Simpson Grant yes Ulysses Simpson Grant just what I say, he was not to be any way what he did. He sat as anybody can see. Perhaps he stood which need not be if he did not want to. Hiram Ulysses stood, he did not sit, he stood which was just as well as he was just as well to stand.

They do not lean they do not walk they do not run they do not talk but everything they do is that. Often it looks as if everything else was there there in American religion but is everything else there. No everything else has no place there because if there is no sky. Well do not be silly. Lizzie you do understand.

You do understand about no sky. Now you do. And about not to die. Yes now you do. Yes of course now you do.

I cannot think of Ulysses Simpson Grant without tears. He was so what shall it be not by any night not by any day not by any light not by any way, but Ulysses Simpson Grant, which one is, that one is, who can come that one can come, for which they come not of for which they come but they can in that case but which they in that case can place, I place him there. Do you too. Do you two place him there which do you do. I do I place him there. I which I place him there, not only for me to be me, I am an American which if which I can be only I know, I know all about sitting and standing but I do not sit and stand in that way not yet nor has been.

Once more I say it all.

They commence as they began, in a way they began.

Oh yes.

And now they will place no one anywhere to stay because no one not they can stay.

Staying is like waiting, there is no staying in American war in American religion in American anywhere.

Ulysses Simpson Grant was a leader in religion was a leader in war only there is no leading there not in American religion not in American war not in American anywhere. Not in that. Waiting, staying, saying, dying has nothing to do with that.

Well as much as Lizzie, well as much will you understand as much this as much.

Ulysses Simpson Grant come before not before as he sat not after or before as he sat but was he killed not he, did he die yes he, but likely as likely for that Ulysses Simpson Grant, U. S. Grant as that.

This is why it is all true this what I have said.

WILBUR WRIGHT

ID he name himself Wilbur because there was another W. This is sometimes done.

Or was he named so, Wilbur Wright.

I once knew a man by the name of Wilbur but nobody knew that that was his name. Everybody who knew him knew him by another name, he knew himself by another name and it was not a name that began with W. He made a completely different name. He said that it had once been his brother's name, not Wilbur but the name he had when everybody knew him, and that his brother was dead. Is it and was he. Nobody who knew him then knew but really it made no difference. At any rate nobody who knew him then knew that he had another name and that name had been Wilbur. There is a reason why not.

It came out quite by accident that Wilbur was his name. Not by accident but because it had to happen. It had to come out officially and so was known that Wilbur was his name Sir.

He was afraid to have Wilbur as a name. He could not come to be what he did not come to be if Wilbur had been his name.

Now do you see what I mean and how much the first name or Christian name can mean. Wilbur Wright was not afraid of his name. He had no reason to be. Wilbur was his name and he had that name and his brother had another name and they both had their names. At least I imagine so or at least I suppose so. Perhaps they had other names too John or Ernest or even Frederick too. But this will not do. It will not do to think that they had other names too.

I only tell this story of Wilbur to show what it means to have a name. Everybody has a name anybody has a name and everybody anybody does what he does with his name feels what he feels about his name, likes or dislikes what he has to have with having his name, in short it is his name unless he changes his name unless he does what he likes what he likes with his name.

Wilbur was his name Wilbur Wright was his name. In a kind of a way nobody that is nobody who thinks about him thinks about him without both of his names which makes one name.

I remember so well hearing about his name I mean the whole of his name Wilbur Wright. Of course I do not remember the exact time when I first heard his name, who would if they were not perfectly interested in airplanes and I am not although I like it and I cannot almost remember the first time I saw one. Only it is a question am I sure whether it was in town or country. I saw one as a first one in the city, the city of Paris and I saw one as the first one in the country around Paris. Both cases were surprising but the one in the country was startling. But before that I had already heard the name of Wilbur Wright the Wright brothers otherwise known as the Wright Brothers and that they kept a bicycle repair shop, which fact was neither startling nor surprising but it was undoubtedly pleasing.

Now all this has to do with. What if Wilbur Wright had been an artist a painter, one who made pictures and perhaps they would have been good pictures too if they naturally had been.

That is if they had naturally been pretty that is as pictures not lovely but very well done and having that kind of meaning the kind of meaning pictures have when pictures are made out of painting, that is by painting, what would he have been.

Let me tell about painters painting and how Wilbur Wilbur Wright would have been if he had been one, which indeed I will think that he has been.

Painting when you paint. I do not know how they are when they paint, nobody knows how they are when they do anything. But I know what they are when they paint and so one can I can know what they are not as they paint but as they are painters.

Do you see the difference if you do not then let me tell you.

But first all I know about Wilbur Wright. As I was saying I heard about Wilbur Wright. I know that and then much later without knowing it was there I saw where they had a monument to him in France that is I accidentally saw it where it was. And that was very nice. It made Wilbur Wright what he was. Did you ever hear about his being an American well I had and it gave me a funny feeling to see his monument there where it was. And why. Because he seemed not to be there where it was. Not at all. Did I not tell you about American American religion, well there you are. Do you see what I mean.

What else did I know about Wilbur Wright. I knew what he looked like and this was not only necessary but usual because it was just all everybody or anybody did then.

And this makes all the difference because I know now what I did know then.

Volume II

AND now I will tell how he painted pictures was a painter and was used to being one.

No he did not paint pictures but he might have and if he had he would have been as he was.

How do you come to be a picture painter and how are you used to being one.

I do not know that he did not paint, he might have and if he had he would have looked as he did, been as he was.

Are painters of pictures anything like actors and what could make them alike. Ah this, ah yes this, and has this anything to do with airplanes that is flying. I think yes and I will make you see or not see what I see what they see. Not say but see yes see.

Actors do not hear themselves when they speak they see themselves when they speak but you know that. Just think of actors and you do or you will know that. Oh yes just alike.

Painters paint pictures and the pictures having been painted they are there that is the pictures are there. The painter having painted the picture he sees it. Now do you see why that makes him just like an actor.

Here let us begin again.

A painter paints a picture and the picture which is there and which he sees there is the picture he has painted. No matter how few or how many pictures there are to paint, those he has painted are the pictures that are there. He sees them there because they are there just always right there, naturally if they have been painted.

That makes him like an actor who no matter how much he speaks always sees himself speak, he does not hear himself speak or if he does it is no matter but he sees himself speak which is what is the matter, which is what does matter.

It is difficult to see what makes them alike actors and painters but I will try again and flyers.

Any actor.

Any painter does not see the picture he has painted it is the picture he has painted which is there and as he is there with it and it is always there with him and why, because it is there beside him. Where else should it be but beside him. And where else should he be. He never is anywhere else. Never at all anywhere, that is never anywhere else. This makes him not alone. No painter or no actor is alone. No flyer is alone. Do you see what I mean.

Why is a painter like an actor. He is just for that reason. Well a writer can be alone because he may have nothing to look at nothing, but not an actor or a painter. Oh no or a flyer oh no.

Now do you see what I mean.

This has nothing to do with American religion nothing at all, it might even not have anything to do with American religion not at all. But Wilbur Wright has something to do with American religion and so all this is this. Everything which is this is not added to this not at all.

And yet he was like that. If you think he was a painter and think slowly he was like that.

Let us begin. Not at all with all. But with Wilbur Wright.

Yes Wilbur. Yes Wright.

Yes Wilbur Wright.

If Wilbur Wright had been a painter just like there are painters American painters would he have been different from what he was. No not at all because painters American painters are like that and I will tell you exactly what I mean.

American flyers are like that and to this we can add Lindbergh. Now slowly you will see what I mean.

American painters when they paint are not painters. Actors when they act are not actors that is American actors that is they are actors but not European actors they are cinema actors and that is an entirely and very different thing. And I will tell you exactly what I mean.

Now I will tell you exactly what I mean.

There is a very important difference between actors and cinema actors and this is the difference between American and European. Oh yes you will know what I mean.

I said and I said it well I said an actor sees what he says. Now think a little how he looks and how he hears what he sees. He sees what he says. Now think about a cinema actor. They have not that to be that they are like American painters, they are American painters and they are American flyers. And what are American painters like, I will tell you because I have watched them paint.

What are Americans like. I tell you I will tell you. While and awhile and I will I will tell you.

All this has to do with American religion with American with Wilbur Wright with Wilbur and with everything and with alright. Now listen carefully while I tell you how American painters paint and as they find they are not like European painters who paint. European painters who paint are extended to the pictures after the pictures have been painted, they are in so much like European actors who see what they say. This is the difference. Now about American painters. To-day yesterday or any day. How do they do it.

They do it like this.

When they paint it does not make any difference what gets upon the canvas, they are they and they feel that they are going to be they. Oh yes. They. They are they. That is what they look like and that is what they feel. Anybody who sees them do it knows what they do.

This is the way they are all through and that makes them not at all like actors who see what they say it makes them like photographs, cinematographs that is actors who know not what they are but where they are. A European actor does not know where they are or when they are they know if they see what they hear. Of course they see they always see. They hear to see. By this I mean yes this.

Now what has this to do with Wilbur Wright. Well it has a lot to do with Wilbur Wright.

I will begin all over again in a minute.

There are two things to make clear each time. Actors and cinema actors.

Painters and actors.

American painters.

American flyers.

Do you see how twos are twos.

But anybody might see that.

When an American painter paints does it matter really matter where his canvas is or where his paints. Not if after all he is certain to know that it is there where he has been that he is not to be. That makes it mean that as he looks he does not see. Why should he see. Between you and me why should he see. If he were to see would he not look and if he were to look would he not have to care if he were or were not there and he does not have to, no indeed he does not have to. And why. Because in American religion no one does die. And so why should he see, why should he look why should there be any difference there if he can do what there is to do there. He has that not to see but to be. Oh yes you see what I mean. Nobody can get excited about that.

I think I remember exactly how they can look not to see not to be but why, because in American religion no one is to die. Any one can be killed or taken away. So much for that.

I know exactly their expression the expression of an American painter when he paints and it is exactly the same expression as an American flyer when he flies, and the same thing but that it is not an expression which makes him not like a European actor see what he says.

Oh Lizzie do you do you understand. I wish you would because I do and I wish oh how I wish that you would too.

Lizzie do you understand.

Anyway I know I must begin again to tell you so.

I slowly know that everything is different so, that I can notice it.

Volume III

IT IS very interesting but I have just heard from one and his name is Ulysses. Ulysses Lee. When this you see remember me. And there is nothing more to be said is there. Names call to names as birds call to birds. And sometimes birds come and sometimes names come but not always. Most often they do come even if not always.

There has been no disappointment either about Ivy or Yvonne. The name came and there she is just like that. I now I have convinced all those who said they knew what I said.

Thank you so much, and as for Lizzie thank you so much. An interlude.

This does not really distract my mind from the very great the very vital subject of what is a painter not only while he paints but when he has painted and how would Wilbur Wilbur Wright have this in common. Nobody need yield to that in not making a mistake. There is no mistake, not anything is a mistake in which they mean I mean.

As I was saying a painter having painted he can see what he has painted; not only can he see but he does see and that is so important he does see as he has painted and in as much he is all there all always there as that, that what, that painting, well of course that painting. But you do not understand, naturally and of course not you do not understand. This is European painting and so yes yes you do you do understand.

To come back to the question of American and will we now be left behind. By whom. I might make a joke and say by Mr. Roosevelt but of course yes, yes yes of course to be left behind, but by Wilbur Wright, oh no not yet and there is no smile no no not yet.

Wilbur Wright will not yet left or be left, behind or not behind no not yet not as yet or if ever. Ever is of no importance. Nor which they ask. Because they do not ask. Ask any yet.

What is it to be an American American religion American war and not any more. That would be very sad but not yet if not yet why not yet. Perhaps Wilbur Wright will tell us yet not yet. If he were a painter had been he would have made pictures and he would have been all that he had been. He would have told all he had been and not yet.

Let no one forget that he flew, yes oh yes he did. He did just as he did. It might have been trotting on a horse in a way behind they say behind a horse. The horse trots. It might be that which made an American that. That is what that is. Think well does not mean thinking. Which should an American do, not think. Why not. Because if American religion is all of you who who can think. And why not. They need not arrange why not. Nor need they think if they think, why not, why not think if it is why not. Nobody needs to say why rather than why not. Nobody does or was.

I wish to say simply what I think of Wilbur Wright.

And I also wish to say simply how he would have been had he been a painter which he might have been of course yes if he had painted. It would have been for him a most natural thing.

I think of two things a name, which he had, and a thing which he did.

And what else.

Why and for which what else.

Does anybody know that fly or flying or a flyer means that.

Think well not of any minute nor even of every minute. That has nothing to do with American religion. But it has to do with American flying with American painting with Wilbur Wright.

It is not a sad story not at all a sad story the story of Wilbur Wright. Listen to me while I tell it to you right.

Volume IV

ONCE when they were together they were brother and brother and always at that time they were. There is no trouble either in being any brother because they were together. I do not wish not to mention two but to you I will just mention one and this one was named Wilbur Wright. If he had painted he would have painted, and his brother would he have painted. No his brother would not have painted. Brothers do not paint as brothers and if they do they do not. Now I wonder would they the paintings Wilbur Wright would have painted would they have been like something that was done if it had not been done before. Very likely most very likely. Oh yes without my saying it you do oh yes you do know what I mean. It would not even if it would, have been something like something that had been done before if he had painted, which he did, if he did paint, which he did.

It is just like a detective book. Here we have the parts. Wilbur Wright and he with his brother Orville invented airplaning. Gliding. Do you glide to fly or do you glide and why. Oh yes to fly.

Now then there is painting and being a painter makes you not do thinking but makes you do what you are to see.

Do you see airplanes are up in the sky if there is a sky which there is not. Oh no which there is not. And this makes American painting all the same which if it is which it is not.

Now do you see that Wilbur Wright would have been that and if so would he have looked like that. That is as he did. Yes if he had been an American painter. He would have looked just as much as he did look like he did.

And this makes it easy to see why an American can be just what he can be. Yes indeed I know, I see it I hear it and I tell you so but mostly I know it and you know.

I have just said that it is not so very easy to make anybody see what is inside any head, but all the way beside you have to know what is inside the body just as well to make it so and make it go. Which it does as much as if it is a picture a cinema or an airplane. Oh yes which I think oh yes.

Do you feel how Americans do not die.

Look. When you look what do you see. Nothing. And why do you look like that. Because you look where you are looking at.

But you see something, but what are you looking at if you do or do not have to have it as not be looking at.

Do you see the difference between looking at and looking like that and looking at that.

Anybody can be an American and not know, know at what, or not what you are not looking at.

Yes you see something like that that is the difference like that be-tween that.

A little to be not either yet.

Always you get nearer American not being American but seeing American if you see being American. And like that. Or yet.

Wilbur Wright was a painter who painted pictures and he was like that he looked like that.

When European painters paint pictures they do not look like that they paint like that, not as they look but as they paint and they paint yet. Who sees what any one who has been painting who indeed does or must paint will not paint yet.

How I love to explain.

I feel that which they do they can be to see. And if not.

Remember that mountains are awful if they say where are they but if they say here they are they are still awful but not awful because it is not awful not to say so. Not once not twice.

Exactly twice.

I am getting nearer and nearer Wilbur Wright. Alright. Very well. Alright. Do you see how very well sounds like something but not nearly enough as much like it. Listen to me.

Painting pictures may take place in and by an American.

This is possible.

Oh Wilbur Wright.

And if he does he feels earnestly whatever there is if it is to mention. Oh yes. This is what is as he does and did. Wilbur Wright.

And when he looked like that he did it.

He always looked like that and he always did it and this also which is right, Wilbur Wright. Alright.

What is the difference between a European and an American. I am telling you all so.

Let us get back to painters and painting. You can never hear it enough so.

What are they like.

What are actors like.

What is the difference between whether they care.

Yes they care.

Painters care.

Actors care.

Well even so.

And many more much more so.

Which is what means that there is no ritual. That is for a European to say.

But there are Americans and others. And in all that.

And now I will tell about all that.

Volume V

To COME back to the question of what they did when they did it then.

Listen to me listen to this.

A painter painting pictures makes a picture look like this. And if he does, it makes him desirous to do it again. If he does it again he has done many of them and all of these many are there. And what does he do. He knows it. And if he knows what does he feel. He feels it.

The result of all this is that he does not see it but they and they are all there include himself in them. Now do you see why he is like an actor who sees himself speaking. Yes you do. You do see this and it is important because sooner or later it will make you see everything and if you see everything you are not at all blind and neither is an airplane and neither is Wilbur Wright and neither is an American and this makes the rest so. It changes nothing from up to down or right to left or a moon or anything or partly that. It makes no difference in any arrangement. Now I will tell you what I like.

I like American and American.

Yes I do.

Now see here and listen to me.

If a country is very big is it generous. I do not have to say so. If any airplane flies very high does it have to fly higher. Whichever you say is whichever you say.

There is no use in a definition which defines none of these things nor indeed does not define it wholly. I tell you and I tell you so that is the way a painter paints. A preacher is not like that but an actor is and that makes it necessary for me to tell you why a preacher is not like that. A preacher hears what he says he does not see what he says.

There that seems to you everything.

Lizzie do you understand.

Now to come back to the difference between a European painter and an American painter and how as differently they look as they paint.

And then we will describe Wilbur Wright oh yes we will.

You know what Wilbur Wright looked like even if you never saw him. Anybody could. Anybody and an American could.

Now remember how I say that a country if it is very big can be mean. And they can even say I mean I mean. Not in a kind of a way if they were born there. No not if they were born there.

Listen to this.

I say that America is a large land and it being so they do not have to care because nobody can stare since they are all there so they can be mean. Do you see what I mean. Oh yes you do you do see what I mean.

Once more how does an American paint or look while he is painting and how does a European paint and look while he is painting. Both are like an actor, they see what they say but they do not hear, oh no why should anybody hear. Very likely it is not at all necessary to hear. And yet ears are curious very curious. They do not move up and down but they sometimes do look so. They can look so in a photograph they can even look so in a painting but they cannot look so in real life nor in an airplane, no hardly in an airplane. No I guess not.

Why should Wilbur Wright hesitate about this. He never did. He never did hesitate about this.

Now I know why I try.

I have forgotten all who said they know and see here I know I know why airplanes pictures and actors neither sink nor swim live or die survive or perish. Do you see how the quotation makes them come to like to hear what they say only they do not they see what they say yes sir they do too they see what they say and the reason why is this and this is what I explain. Very much like I did but different quite different quite as different. Oh yes quite. The difference is this. Wilbur Wright perhaps Orville who helped did help invented the airplane. If he had been a picture painter what would he have done.

The events in the life of Wilbur Wright.

Quietly the events in his life.

I do not know that there were any events in the life of Wilbur Wright. Does it make any difference. If not what were they.

He made the glide and all Europe knew about it in a kind of a way they knew it first because as a subject it was not new in Europe and in America well it was not new but it was not nearly so well known. And so quietly there were no events in the life of Wilbur Wright. Which they were not.

And then he was dead. And this was not something that had happened but if it can be said it was one of these things that nobody knew which in itself made no difference.

Wilbur Wright was dead but this was as quiet as everything else and then there it was at once a monument was there for him just as quietly at once.

But in Europe. Yes of course in Europe at Le Mans.

All this made it be alright. Yes well yes alright.

Now suppose he had been a painter a painter of pictures. And how does a flyer feel does he see how he moves or does he not or does he not see how he moves and if he does what does he see.

That is to say what does he see if he moves and if he flies does he move. Which does he do.

Wilbur Wright saw how he moved. He did not so much gather to move as he saw how he moved.

That is what he saw and if he had painted pictures would this have been what he had to see. No one can wonder what there is to see if they are there which they can be.

Oh yes do you see now what that has to do with a painter what that has to do with an actor what that has to do with Wilbur Wright.

I am going to describe everything I know about painting about American painting about European painting and then you will know all that there is about Wilbur Wright.

Also in between you will know something about what is American. Every little while you will get to know something about what is American.

I may not say I forget because it is not that but I love to go away. Oh do not love me to go away. I just say do not love me just to go away.

Now then hear then what I say of them.

There is nothing then that anybody can relive then that is Wilbur Wright because he was alright. Oh yes.

He was just right.

Nobody could be anxious.

Once there was winning his way but this never amounted to that.

No it did not I say did not, amount to that.

Wilbur Wright was just there as that. How do you like it.

Oh come to be here with me.

It is very soon to know that Wilbur Wright was so and did not feel that it was best to help it.

Volume VI

Once they asked a painter did he see what he saw and he said not alike.

Now I always like to think of Wilbur Wright not seeing what he saw. He saw how he moved. Yes. Yes.

It made no difference not to Wilbur Wright if it was or if it was not alike not if he moved.

If he moved he saw he moved.

Well not as a doubt.

How can you doubt if you see how you move.

But did he move or did he see he moved and if saw did he see it again. Oh yes he did.

And so he began to be where he had been. Is it true about bicycles. In as much as that yes.

And this makes it American if so.

But they see so if not not to move so.

There is no need to see to move. But he did see not to move but what it is to move. Oh yes he saw.

How many acts are there in moving. And this makes them feel better.

He sees when he moves.

He sees how he moves.

He sees moving.

Can you do you see.

When this you see remember me this has this had nothing to do with Wilbur Wright.

He never was told which is the same as taught that.

When a painter paints he does not have to see what he has painted but he looks like that that is it which is painted looks like that. That is a deception but they like to please deceive. Not a painter painting not a flyer flying not an actor acting oh no not at all. They do not like to deceive nor do they deceive.

Which is what they do not do.

Why do I think these things are different from other things and also American. Because I do. And really so I do. So do you too.

For which I know why I tell you so.

They look different when they do so when they paint and when they fly there Europeans when they try. Oh yes they do.

You to me.

But they know where they are American from which they are American.

What did he say.

He knew what I said.

It is slowly getting on.

Volume VII

WILBUR WRIGHT was not remarkable as a painter but he had no one to remind or to remember, that is what he did. He came to do as much. By this I mean this.

He did not remember bicycles being a painter why did he. Bicycles had the form of bicycles and were not needed because he had had whatever bicycles or he had needed.

If he painted, then he had what neither he nor bicycles had not needed, that is to say he needed not to repair bicycles but anything he did was that.

When he painted what did he paint. He did not paint bicycles he painted pictures and they were like that. No need to tell me how or what he did. No need at all.

What I wish to say is this.

It is not only unlike but it is very much like what they do that they should do not only what it is they do but not what they have left. Wilbur Wright left bicycles but bicycles were not left, they never are, left behind. He did not leave painting behind but that alone made no difference. Let me have no choice or rather a choice of assemble.

What is a painting. A painting is something seen after it has been done and in this way left alone nobody can say he or I left it alone. No painting is left alone. This is not possible. Insofar as it is a painting it is not left alone. Now do you begin to see about Wilbur Wright or do you not and if not why do you not if as you know very well just what Wilbur Wright was.

A painting insofar as it is a painting not being left alone because this could not be. If it is a painting it could not be left alone. Neither could it be left alone. Now how about an airplane now how about it. And how about Wilbur Wright and what he looked like that is what it is if he was it which he was.

Do you begin to see how a painting being a painting is never left alone. Now has this anything to do with an actor or an airplane now has it. Is it a bicycle that is like that. Well perhaps no perhaps yes perhaps.

Anyway if Wilbur Wright was right and he was right he was connected with a bicycle and painting and an airplane and none of these three even when they were alone were as it were left alone. I know so well what I mean. They say not but I do. I know so well you know so well well yes know so well what it is. And naturally I mean what it is just as anybody would do anybody would mean just as well what it was. If they listen quietly nobody can be quiet when they listen but this has nothing to do with Wilbur Wright which makes it say so. Or words to that effect.

What I mean is this. Wilbur Wright like an American should did not mind that no painting even when it was alone was not left alone that no airplane when it was left alone was not left alone and perhaps a bicycle too, but better not or rather just as well not.

Wilbur Wright was an American in respect to which it was that he

was there and not only not that but not there that is to say there when
a painting which was alone was not left alone. That made him do what
he did do or rather be what it was he was which was a painter oh yes a
painter. One who painted one who had painted or who would have
painted a picture. Yes a picture. An American who painted a picture
and an American if he left but there is nothing to leave how can you
leave, care for care and how can no one care but of course which they
do not. Think how nobody has pride and tried. Very important. Think
of that and then remember all about Wilbur Wright oh yes of course
yes oh yes of course yes you do.

I wish to tell you how not to explain what you do not see.

Wilbur Wright painted a picture not only one no one can any one
only paint one. No not of course not.

Which one does it.

Wilbur Wright can paint any picture he painted and if when he did
he did not stop that did not come to be the same thing nor in any place.

Oh I could almost weep, weep means to be very sorry that no picture
can be left alone. But that is natural because a picture has been painted
and the painting is paint.

Now does everybody see.

All who have all have remembered no last.

No is not what is said but has to do with pride and tried. You who
see that do see that.

Volume VIII

I WILL carefully describe pictures not so carefully airplanes not carefully at all bicycles and quite carefully Wilbur Wright.

This makes it just right.

Now at last I am freed from the oppression of checks.

Everybody can think of going to school. Even which they did if
most of the time they did not go there and very likely Wilbur Wright
did not.

There is no necessity why everybody should thank them for a school.
But everybody can and does. Can who does. Does he go to school if he
is sent.

How many American boys do not go to school and this is perhaps why they cannot like it. They cannot like anything in which they need to have theirs as a request.

American boys are that you might say like that if you wish to use the word like but it is not necessary.

Requesting is not important in an American and going to school is a request. Any boy can leave nothing, much alone. And so he came gravely he came, he might have been there when he came. No one can know that they know that Wilbur Wright came neither as early or as late as it was at all necessary to use as much obliged. He meant to come when he was there. After all how can anybody do anything in a day.

Every day they were not to wait. And this brings me so near to nearly and not to that.

They did make their glide. For which they came.

Remember that there is a monument in his honour.

Volume IX

WILBUR WRIGHT I do not even know whether Wilbur Wright was married. I do not even know if he was ever married. And in a kind of a way it would make a difference both as to his having gone to school and as to his ever having been married. He certainly had not been indifferent to being married and if he had married he would have married young but it is just as well that he was not.

Just here I can introduce this about a wife.

There is no use in denying a wife is not only pleasant but useful. Never never do you want not to be grateful for having a wife. It is a thing for which always there is to be an expressed gratitude. And why. Because a wife is irremediably what is necessary not only with and will but in season and in out. There is no out season. No out season in a wife. Now you might think all of this is not true but it is.

It is of course natural that Wilbur Wright might have had a wife and daughters but I do not believe that he had. I really do not believe it.

I believe that he went to school but that he did not very much enjoy it, he liked it oh yes he liked it but it was not an all day occupation. A school can only be that if one is not apt to be left and Wilbur Wright was not the kind any one left.

It was not a secret service to leave him of course it was not.

Just by that much was he like that.

How often is it necessary never to see anybody.

Some people know just how often but Wilbur Wright was not like that.

He did not an American did not leave did not leave nothing alone. How can you leave nothing alone just tell me that.

Wilbur Wright might of and he did paint pictures.

Neither he nor they were left alone.

All alone.

I may be right but if I am I am not right all alone. Wilbur Wright.

Volume X

How many days and wages does it take to make it alone.

That is a question to ask.

Volume XI

WHAT I like about yesterday is that they all say what they used to say and they all go away like they used to go away.

Oh yes they do.

No one exchanges this at any time. They used it and they use it often but not at all to cause any one any difficulty at once or even oftener.

And now what am I talking about.

I am talking about how if there were a history it would be the same and in a kind of a way there can never be a history because indeed it can never not be the same. And so question me, say that you like and you look like me and that you look at me. No one can question Wilbur Wright for me.

All this is not a puzzle.

Now I wish to explain.

Having never seen Wilbur Wright he does not look alike but

certainly and surely he does. Not only when he went to school and did not care about it and why do they know it because it is just like it. He does look alike and even later. Yes even to-day which is not as different as yesterday because to-day is not lighter.

Now who does he look like. Well any one that is anybody knows that too. Yes you do. You know what he looks like. Is that the same as you know whom he looks like. Is it the same or is it not.

Who can answer and what.

Well I can answer it is and it is not.

All this is the most important thing about Wilbur Wright. Just the most important thing about Wilbur Wright. All this is.

I will continue how I know what I know. I feel like that.

But would he be careful about not or about being at school when he was a boy and if he were would it have made any difference.

There is a funny thing about this, if they are earnest and interested they may like to go to school or they may not.

Does or was is very pretty and it may be just the same or it may be very different and not any one to blame but they do blame some one, some do, but if they do it is not at all important.

Not even for them to them.

However one thing is certain whether Wilbur Wright did or did not go to school and like school makes more difference if he was to be a maker of his glide than if he was to be a painter of his pictures and the reason why is this.

Now in both cases as I told you a painter paints and the painting painted being there makes him the painter be in connection with his painting which is in connection with the thing painted and it all being there, having been there he is not only there but more there. And so why did he go to school. But of course why not. Why did he not go to school neither one is at all important.

Now on the other hand to make the glide Wilbur Wright had to feel that he would know where he was when he moved and for this it might be not important but necessary that he had been to school or if not that he had not been to school. Now then how could he be both. Wilbur Wright could be could be both and that is the reason and because of this reason he is rightly was rightly named Wilbur Wright. Does and was.

Does and was is not only not very easy but also not what he asked. But he had what he asked.

He glided.

Anybody who can remember about Wilbur Wright knows this which is Wilbur Wright.

Nobody knew he asked. And this was true he never had asked. You can see by his photograph that he never had asked.

Volume XII

He might have been not young not so very young to glide. He was not as a matter of fact any age to glide. There is no age to glide. He was not young and if he had been young had he. That might have been something to ask but in his case he that is it was not to ask, or asked. It had nothing to do with that it had to do with what he and his brother did. They did neither better nor worse than that. Even occasionally.

I like to think of Wing and Wing but they did not. I like to think of the Wept of the Wish ton wish but they also did not. And if they did. All this I do not know because it might be so. Indeed it might be so. But it was not. If not why not. Ah that you know.

But this has nothing to do with pictures of course it has nothing to do with pictures with pictures or tears for pictures or why they were as they were dressed. Think of Secret Service. Who can moan about secret service or yes.

Not Wilbur Wright although he might as he looked. He was not alone as he looked.

So then think readily why Wilbur Wright was as he saw in his pictures.

Listen to this alright.

For them they place.

Wilbur Wright as I was saying could not be remembered now because a great many have not seen his photograph have not heard his wishes have not seen him now nor even know that he made pictures. Oh yes they do. They do not know about it.

He never said it was a hard thing to do, or harder than that, harder than what he did do.

I can see him so easily.

Not saying that he knew that he did do what he did do.

Oh yes of course yes.

Wilbur Wright oh yes of course yes.

America. They need not be known to be.

Yes yes now I have made something out of nothing. So did he.

Yes yes. So did we.

Listen while I tell about it further. And this includes how to go to school.

I always come back to that, this includes how to go to school.

Which Wilbur Wright did. More or less.

Which he liked or which he did not like. And this is not more or less. Because for instance did he want to be taught by his teacher. A great many do not, a great many like Wilbur Wright do not. Perhaps he did not and perhaps he did. If he did he did and if he did not he did not.

That is the way it was and it made no difference whether he was older or younger than his brother. Probably he was older he almost certainly or always was.

After he went to school he was quite active. Quite as active as that. By active I mean that he was very quiet and moved a great deal. Not so much from here to there but where he was. He was at no time disturbed by anything disagreeable.

He always kept as still as he was not still but quiet as he was.

He always with always remembering that there were two no one could separate the two from one.

Do you realise how much this is what they were.

Wilbur Wright, Orville Wright is still alive.

Wilbur Wright which is what they meant by a picture. In his photograph he looked like that, he was very busy being made like that, and pictures of course pictures would be made like that, and Secret Service of course any secret service would be made like that.

How do pictures look when they are made. They do not look as if they have been made but they look as they look if they have been made.

By this I mean. Once a picture has been made any one making a picture has made a picture and so having made a picture they will look about. As they look about the picture looks about and as they all look about they all look together and nobody looks alike. This made Wilbur Wright glide.

An American painter is not just like that. He can can he yes he can leave a picture alone.

Wilbur Wright was mentioned honourably mentioned by all who came to know his name.

Anybody could feel about him like that.

If he looked like that anybody could feel about him like that.

And he did.

Which they did.

I wish to explain about hope.

What has hope got to do with pictures.

Nothing. Not anything.

Wilbur Wright never had to hope.

That you see made him see.

And so no pictures needed to be seen.

No pictures he did.

If he saw nothing, that had nothing to do with not looking.

Observe that.

Nevertheless it did have nothing at all to do with that.

Wilbur Wright had made all possible.

All possible does not leave anything to itself. And no picture can be left to itself. If it were left to itself nobody would be around.

But he flew.

He did not have it to do.

So much more is it important to care. Not only to care but to care for the picture. The picture cannot care, you cannot care. Wilbur Wright can not care. Only when they can be careful then anybody can care.

This makes Wilbur Wright a triumph.

He was not triumphant he was not as he looked but he looked as he felt we felt that he looked as he felt.

We felt alone. He was alone.

Nobody left to feel.

Which made which they chose possible.

They were not only left they were not only not waiting they were not only not careless they were not only prepared and careful. So we may say that.

Volume XIII

ALL this that is this is about pictures. And Wilbur Wright painting and having painted them.

Volume XIV

How can you change anything when you have seen everything. Not that he could look because he could not. One thing is to look and as you look not to look away. That is one thing and it is very likely not what Wilbur Wright did. If he had done so he would have known, and this he did know that if there has once been a revolution there is no need and if there is a need there is no time to make another one. And so he died. But this is not at all what I wished to say. I wished to say that he knew how he did what he did and this had no reference whatsoever to one day or another day. That and that is really certain that was Wilbur Wright's way.

It did not make him have a brother but he did have a brother but having all that they were together. This had nothing to do with painting pictures. There Wilbur Wright was alone as is or is not well known.

What did he do when he did paint a picture and what he did do when he did not paint a picture. But he always did paint a picture because this which he did was what he saw. And once what he saw he saw no more although for all that he continued to soar. Oh yes why often do they wish. They wish me not and not for what. Do not complain of wish.

Wilbur Wright managed ordinarily and fairly to be there where he did and was. He managed fairly and ordinarily.

They need not complain of in between.

No one need to since there was no hope of a miscarriage. How could there be with care. And care did not make him careful. He managed just with that.

I liked to hear what they say but they did not need it for him. That made it especially for him what he did. He died. Not while he died.

Not nearly as much died as dead. Not nearly as much dead. Not nearly. No not nearly. Why he died.

May we care to believe that no one went anywhere.

Think not of which way but where did he go.

This does not make him be heard but be known.

If he went up and down or forward and back, if he had known how bicycles are made and mended, if he had been as quiet as he looked and as quick, if he had been as they saw then every one who knew him said the same. Oh yes nobody tells what he likes or what he is like. It is not necessary because just think how he looked in his photograph. Just think of that. You all know just think of that.

It is of no importance that he died, just think of that but nevertheless we know and knew and so did he too. Just like that.

Know what he did.

Now to come back. Not back but to come to why if he walked he did not run and he did not run he walked, and if he did not walk there it was as if he stood and there he stood. Any way it is not necessary not at all necessary to say.

To say what he did because everybody knows that.

Please do not be bereft of anything. Bereft for him had no meaning. That is in its way a beginning.

I think easily not of why they died or why they lied. Not he either or one.

Nobody can know better than any one and he was one.

Do you see begin to see what it means to be that he painted and if he did not who did. Not he certainly not he. Just like his going to school. Not he certainly not he.

But there never is no for no an answer.

And so he painted why yes he did. He painted three his pictures. Pictures for a picture.

Volume XV

NEED he be wounded by anything.

No he need not.

Volume XVI

I OFTEN wondered what he needed twice.

Volume XVII

WHAT did he need twice. His brother. No not his mother.

If he had painted a picture he would have needed it once or twice but not oftener. Not even ever oftener.

And then it came to be, I will not say it came to pass that he did not have to go but as he came not to pass but to be there no one was astonished by astonished I mean surprised to see him.

It was natural to see him just as it was natural to have seen him have him.

He had himself and this was as natural as being where he was up there.

If he was there he was up there.

Not to any one or to any questioning.

He could tell why one thing any thing came to have that be any thing. Not be one thing because he was not elbowed or allowed.

Remember where he came when he came.

And any moment that came.

No fault of any one any thing.

Not for which it or he was known.

Need height be a height.

Need or need white be a white.

In either way he used neither. Neither in his talking in his flying or in his painting.

And why not.

Because no circumstances no kind of circumstances made why not.

Do you begin to see how readily or not readily or reading regularly or not I see.

It is to see why by time.

I can remember that if it was wonderful it was natural.

Let me arrange everything about a picture.

His picture.

Which was his picture.

Any picture which was painted by him.

Volume XVIII

IF ANYBODY knew just what he had to do.

This never could be said of Wilbur Wright.

I wish now anxiously to care about just what was his share and would he could he do it alone.

This is all a thing to ask not a question to ask but a thing to ask and as it is not a question there is no answer to it.

If Wilbur Wright had done what he did alone he would also have painted pictures because it is like this.

If he had done what he did alone he would have not told it to any one not even while or when it was done because in being done he would have gone on. That would have made him one who was alone when anything was done. He was never alone. This is what made him different from what he was and made it possible that as soon as he was dead they made a monument to him.

I wish everybody could understand this. They would then see the importance as well as the unimportance of being alone. Alone I did it. This can never be said of Wilbur Wright but it might have been said of him if he had been different and what he had done had been differently done but it was not true of him there were always two of which he was one.

Let him think what this means but he does not think what this means nor did he.

I have again seen pictures that he has not painted.

What is a painter, a painter is one who paints pictures and these pictures having been painted he must paint other pictures because he has seen those pictures the ones he has painted, the pictures he has painted. That makes a painter not spared by his pictures but spared by his brother and so Wilbur Wright did not do so, he did not paint pictures not as he might have done if he had only been one.

I am no longer interested in his not having painted one since to have painted one he would have had to paint many of them and to paint many of them he would have had to be one of one and he was not he was one of two.

Oh yes he was he was one of two and this was what he had to do. This is undoubtedly true.

Now for the rest just the real history of Wilbur Wright from the time he looked as he did.

Volume XIX

IF Wilbur Wright let us fancy that Wilbur Wright was born.

To some it is astonishing to have been born. To some it is a puzzle that they can remember everything except the having been born. Gradually no one knows about it.

Did he and if not he did any one know about it.

Wilbur Wright did not mention it did not mention having been born. And why not. Because he was never alone. If one is never alone one does not mention having been born. He was never alone at least not in that way. Anybody knowing that knew what he looked like, at least in his photograph.

They knew how he was not ever alone no not in that way.

After that he went to school and in school he might or he might not care. But at any rate he could remember that although most probably that was not what he did. He most probably did not remember that. A great many who know they are at school when they go to school do not remember that. Most likely he did that well enough he remembered well enough while he was at school that he was at school. At least he looked as if he might have remembered it well enough while he is at school. He looked well enough like that later in his photograph.

He may have liked being at school and he may not. A great many who look like that the way he looks in his photograph do not like being at school when they are at school and being taught by the teachers who teach those who are in the school. A great many who look like he looks in his photograph do like well enough even very well enough to be in school when they are in school and when they are being taught by the teachers who are teaching while they are in school. A great many do not stay in school long enough, do not stay away from school long enough not to like, not not to like being in school while they are in the school where they are being taught by the teachers who are teaching them.

Wilbur Wright went to school enough. He was not particularly alone. No he was not particularly alone.

Later on he was not particularly alone. Later on when he was dead he was not particularly alone he had a monument to him. No he was not particularly alone. He did not look particularly alone no not in his photograph although some who look as he looked in his photograph look as if they were particularly alone. He did not. In spite of all he did not.

Then they glided up and down, not up but down not down but up. Oh yes they glided and he looked alone he looked alone in his photograph. But he was not particularly alone although he looked alone in his photograph.

How do you do is not only said to dogs. This was not the only thing he said because he did not talk like that. This was not his way.

After a while everybody knew it. And it always was just the same, not only for him but immediately that he was dead. Which they all know. And they know why they all say so. He was not particularly alone either. To know how he looked in his photograph.

For which no mention is made as no one says.

I come to think how to-morrow in this country, in the country they will remember him, they will remember about him.

It would take him many years of painting, or which made no difference, it would make no difference if it took many years for painting and still then it would make no difference.

And the reason for this is this.

If any one paints a picture he can see the picture he has painted and he can see it whenever he can look at it and if he has it why can he not look at it, there is no reason for his not looking at it once he has painted it and so he does look at it. And the consequence is that he knows how the picture looks the picture which he has painted.

It is not astonishing that after that he paints a picture again and once again he sees the picture he has painted and that does not complete anything nor complicate anything but it commences to come to be something that can not be left again.

Left, left, left right left, I had a good job and I left left left left right left.

And so you see a great many years would have been just the same. But he glided and not for a great many years oh no not for a great many years.

And so we nearly see Wilbur Wright as he was when he was a painter and any painter is like that quite exactly and very exactly just like that. He cannot be different from like that and this makes no one who paints a picture paint anything because the picture having been painted it is a picture.

How do you do can be said regularly to a dog and he will always respond but not a painter not a painter of a picture.

Do you see why Wilbur Wright continued to be right and why once that he did what he did he died. He did not mean to die. Some do not die but they live again to do it again. He did not.

Nevertheless there is more to it than this. There is beside Wilbur Wright as he looked in his photograph.

I can so well remember just what happened just what would happen if as everybody did, everybody did see how he looked in his photograph.

He never made more than that he never made less than that. He made that. Almost at once he made that.

It is very curious, it does not come either slowly or fast, it does not come either not at all or a little but there it is everybody has the same everybody has the same photograph has seen the same photograph.

This has nothing to do with his having painted a picture and yet in a way it has, not the photograph, but everybody having seen the same photograph.

If you paint a picture you need not live long because if after a while there are two two are not new. Yes pictures are well enough alone. But do not forget Wilbur Wright never was alone, not he, he never never was alone. And why not. Because of course not.

If you have painted a picture you are never alone because finally not at all nobody can tell anything apart not you nor I nor nobody knows, where peas and beans and barley grows. No not, of course not.

And so how often could Wilbur Wright not die. Just often enough. If he had been a painter what would he have had to do.

He would have had to do just what he did and he did, he did do just what he did. And this did not make any matter, that is to say if he went fast or if he went at last it did amount not to the same but not to any difference. He made it all. All is almost enough.

Enough said.

If he had been a painter he would not have had to die and so he would not have been dead and he would not have had a photograph of himself for all to see not he.

Volume XX

I BEGAN by thinking that these that do paint a picture or act a play are alike and I was not mistaken. In each case why they were has no interest, when they were has no interest, how they were has no interest but that they were not alone has an interest. It makes them not two nor not one but it makes them not alone. And so if Wilbur Wright was tried he was not tried by what he did. He did not have to see what he did because he did not look. Do you see why he did not look. Of course you do see why he did not look.

Nevertheless I do see why a painter and an actor and Wilbur Wright were alike. Because they did not have to see when they look, they did not have to look when they see because after all they are all included in alike and in that. How do they move. They do not move from here to there. No not at all. Not at all. Not at all.

They do not move from here to there, not a painter not an actor not Wilbur Wright.

I wonder if you all see that at which you look.

Rest well with that.

Volume XXI

WHY do they close what they open, why do they wish what they leave, why do they connect what they establish why do they die when they fly. Oh yes nobody knows and yet everybody knows that he Wilbur Wright did not die, he did not die because he did or because he did not fly. I wish no one to mean this.

Connect this with every six.

I often think that if he had never done anything except paint except paint pictures would it all have come to this.

If he had painted pictures would he have been quite as much not alone. No not quite as much. And what difference would that have made. It would have made some difference in his photograph. It would also have made some difference in when he died. It would also have made some difference in how he lived. And would it have made some difference in how he was known. Yes it would have made some difference. And would it have made some difference in how he knew himself. Yes it would also in respect to how he knew himself it would have made some difference. Would he have known himself better or worse or not as well. This I do not know. For this I have no answer.

It is not only necessary but it is more than reasonable that Wilbur Wright was such a one as he may wish. He was as he was, such a one.

No one can know anything better than he knew in knowing himself as such a one.

And so not quietly if you like but really if you like, yes really if you like as well as not quietly if you do not like, he was one, and almost then he was one, and not one of two. But he was one of two. Exactly so.

When they were with them they were not without them neither one of either one of them.

He thought Wilbur Wright thought that he was as old as he looked in his photograph. He did not look as old as he looked in his photograph. He was young to look as old as he looked in his photograph. And the occasion for this is this.

He had lived the life he lived the two of them either one of either of them so that when it was done it was not only done but smoothly done and either one of them knew which one. If they did not nobody suffered.

What is suffering.

Suffering is certain is being certain that some time later if anything is lost, that is to say if it is difficult to go on nobody will join in. That is suffering.

That never happened to them. No indeed that did not happen to them.

Any one whom they did not like they did not know. Nobody could call that suffering.

Nobody who lost anything could come to ask either one of them to find anything. You cannot call that suffering.

No one who arranges what they have has it given to them. No indeed you can not call that really suffering.

Whatever you mean you can like or not like to mean. No no one neither one can speak of anything as having anything in it more peaceably than suffering.

And so there was no excuse for just tried. There was no excuse either for just cried.

In this way they the two of them gained everything.

Do you remember how a photograph of Wilbur Wright looked. I do.

Wait a way for just died.

Volume XXII

THE last thing I have to say about painting pictures is this.

Volume XXIII

IN BETWEEN acting painting and flying, in between gliding suffering and tidying, in between, is there anything hazardous in between or are they mixed up with liking or are they not.

Listen to him here only, and this is the occasion of this, nobody can or has heard him.

That is what there is to say.

Feel that as a photograph or a paragraph is. Nobody has heard him.

Them or him. Then or him. Nobody has ever heard him then. Think of a photograph for him or them or then. And cries, he cries, not for himself or for remembering or even for gliding. There is all that difference between tries and cries and tears come then oh yes tears come then.

And so Wilbur Wright is fine.

For which if not only is but it also is not a blessing.

Feel how he feels well. No one but can see this in a photograph.

That makes it sure or surely that if there was no right there was no Wilbur Wright and has is what it is as.

For this reason I wish not to finish as it is or has been begun.

Wilbur fortunately for him Wright fortunately for him Wilbur Wright fortunately for him has been or has not been forgotten.

Believe me or not as you like.

There is a great difference between partly or parcels. And this is so nearly according to what it is as Wilbur Wright. Believe me or not for perplexity.

I wish to say that Wilbur Wright known or Wilbur Wright, Wilbur Wright is not unknown, Wilbur Wright may be right, if not certainly it is or will be they must separate will be from was.

Can you slowly gather whether Wilbur Wright was or is where this or was is here.

For which in might they be in union.

Is there not one. Is there not two.

Is there not one but two. Any photograph of one is not a photograph of two. And so often pleases faces as more. But I do like out loud, Wilbur Wright out loud although he moved but never spoke, not in his photograph.

Wilbur Wright should by any chance he earned or changed as they did not he did. They did immediately make a stone monument to him and they called it Wilbur Wright and no one started or astonished or named or were not known. If it had not been done then would it ever have been done. May be it would but I doubt it but this does nor would make any difference in his photograph.

Wilbur Wright invented. Should they be sad or sadder. Not at all, nor tall nor taller probably he was not tall. But this was not certain no not in his photograph.

I wish to say all I have to say about Wilbur Wright or Wright.

Volume XXIV

I COULD be careful not to cry.

Volume XXV

WILBUR WRIGHT.

Volume XXVI

I COULD be also as very careful not to try not to cry.

As for Wilbur Wright I could be very careful not by this not to try to cry and not to. Because for this if I was careful. I was as careful not to cry.

Wilbur Wright as careful. He was as careful. Wilbur Wright was careful.

Make it that I am not to try to cry.

Mind how I make it.

I will not only saddle safely as plain as well yes or well well not to try.

If it could be used not to cry.

Wilbur Wright for which, better not whether or better for which not to forget for which Wilbur Wright had better not be for which they might cry.

Never separate for which and Wilbur Wright.

He had no reason to try.

I have no reason to cry.

Which is which.

HENRY JAMES

WHAT is the difference between Shakespeare's plays and Shakespeare's sonnets.

I have found out the difference between Shakespeare's plays and Shakespeare's sonnets. One might say I have found out the difference by accident, or one might say I have found out the difference by coincidence.

What is the difference between accident and coincidence.

An accident is when a thing happens. A coincidence is when a thing is going to happen and does.

Duet

AND so it is not an accident but a coincidence that there is a difference between Shakespeare's sonnets and Shakespeare's plays. The coincidence is with Before the Flowers of Friendship Faded Friendship Faded.

Who knew that the answer was going to be like that. Had I told that the answer was going to be like that.

The answer is not like that. The answer is that.

I am I not any longer when I see.

This sentence is at the bottom of all creative activity. It is just the exact opposite of I am I because my little dog knows me.

Of course I have always known Shakespeare's plays. In a way I have always known Shakespeare's sonnets. They have not been the same. Their not being the same is not due to their being different in their form or in their substance. It is due to something else. That something else I now know all about. I know it now but how did I come to know it.

These things never bothered me because I knew them, anybody who knows how to read and write knows them.

It is funny about reading and writing. The word funny is here used in the double sense of amusing and peculiar.

Some people of course read and write. One may say everybody reads and writes and it is very important that everybody should.

Now think everybody think with me, how does reading and writing agree, that is with you. With almost everybody it agrees either pretty well or very well.

Now let me tell a little story. Once upon a time there were a great many people living and they all knew how to read and write. They learnt this in school, they also learnt it when anybody taught it. This made them not at all anxious to learn more. But yet they were as ready to learn more as they ever had been.

There were some who knew that it was very like them, they might have said, very like themselves, to know how to read and write, and they knew too that not everybody could do it.

Do you see what I mean.

Everybody can read and write because they learn how and it is a natural thing to do. But there are others who learn how, they learn how to read and write, but they read and write as if they knew how.

Now one of these who had just come to read and write as if he knew how, said, oh yes, I knew them, I knew them before they knew how to read and write.

I could if I liked mention the names of all of these people. I could mention the name of the one who said he had known them before they knew how to read and write. I could mention the names of the ones he knew before they knew how to read and write.

Shakespeare's plays were written, the sonnets too were written.

Plays and Shakespeare's sonnets. Shakespeare's sonnets and Before the Flowers of Friendship Faded Friendship Faded. Now the point is this. In both cases these were not as if they were being written but as if they were going to be written. That is the difference between Shakespeare's plays and Shakespeare's sonnets. Shakespeare's plays were written as they were written. Shakespeare's sonnets were written as they were going to be written.

I now wish to speak very seriously, that is to say, I wish to converse, I did so, that is I did converse after I had made my discovery. I conversed very seriously about it.

In reading and writing, you may either be, without doubt, attached to what you are saying, or you may not. Attached in the sense of being connected to it.

Supposing you know exactly what you say and you continue to say it. Supposing instead you have decided not to continue to say what you say and you neither do nor do not continue to say it. Does it or does it not make any difference to you whether you do continue to say it.

That is what you have to know in order to know which way you may or may not do it, might or might not do it, can or cannot do it. In short which way you come or do not come to say what you say. Certainly in some way you say what you say. But how. And what does it do, not to you, but what does it do. That is the question.

Shakespeare's plays were written. The sonnets too were written.

Anything anybody writes is written.

Anything anybody reads has been written.

But if anything that anybody writes is written why is it that anybody writing writes and if anybody writing writes, in whom is the writing that is written written.

That is the question.

This brings me to the question of audience of an audience.

What is an audience.

Everybody listen.

That is not an audience because will everybody listen. Is it an audience because will anybody listen.

When you are writing who hears what you are writing.

That is the question.

Do you know who hears or who is to hear what you are writing and how does that affect you or does it affect you.

That is another question.

If when you are writing you are writing what some one has written without writing does that make any difference.

Is that another question.

Are there, is there many another question. Is there.

On the other hand if you who are writing know what you are writing, does that change you or does it not change you.

That is that might be an important question.

If you who are writing know what it is that is coming in writing, does that make you make you keep on writing or does it not.

Which guess is the right guess or is there not a guess yes.

That too is very important.

Perhaps you may say they had it written, they thought they had it written and you thought so more than that you know so, and so in writing that you write is as they thought so, or perhaps as they know so.

Does that make it like that.

Perhaps yes perhaps no.

There are so many ways of writing and yet after all there are perhaps only two ways of writing.

Perhaps so.

Perhaps no.

Perhaps so.

There is one way the common way of writing that is writing what you are writing. That is the one way of writing, oh yes that is one way of writing.

The other way is an equally common way. It is writing, that is writing what you are going to be writing. Of course this is a common way a common way of writing. Now do you or how do you make a choice. And how do you or do you know that there are two common ways of writing and that there is a difference between.

It is true that there is a difference between the one way and the other way. There is a difference between writing the way you are writing and writing the way you are going to be writing. And there is also choosing. There may be a choosing of one way or of the other way.

Now how do you make a choice if you make a choice. Or do you make a choice or do you not make a choice. Or do some do. Or is it true that some do. Or is it true that some do not do so. That some make a choice that some do not do so.

Now if you do how do you make a choice and if you do do make a choice what do you do.

It is true that any one writing and making a choice does choose to write in one of these two ways. They either write as they write or they

write as they are going to write and they may and they may not choose
to do what they are going to do.

If not why not. And if so do they know what they do or do they not.

I am sure you do not understand yet what I mean by the two ways.

I said once when I was seriously conversing, I not only say it but
I think it. By this I mean that I did not choose to use either one of two
ways but two ways as one way.

I mean I do mean that there are two ways of writing.

Once you know that you have written you go on writing. This ex-
plains nothing.

But quite naturally it does not explain because what is it that it does
not explain. Indeed what is it that it does not explain. You can refuse
to explain, when you have written, but what is it that you can refuse
to explain. Oh dear what is it.

You can refuse if you refuse you can refuse to explain when you have
written.

You can explain before and you can explain after and you can even
explain while you are writing. But does that make the two kinds of
writing. No at once I can say not it does not. But and this is or it may
be very exciting or may be not, but in this way you can be and become
interesting. And may be not.

But what is the use of being interesting.

Of course everybody who writes is interesting other wise why would
everybody read everybody's letters.

Do you begin to see does everybody begin to see what this has to do
with Shakespeare's plays and Shakespeare's sonnets. Or do they not.
And if they do begin to see why do they and where do they and how
do they and if they do not do not begin to see why do they not begin
to see. If not why not.

Two ways two ways of writing are not more than one way. They are
two ways and that has nothing to do with being more than one way.
Yes you all begin to see that. There can not be any one who can not
begin to see that. So now there is no use in saying if not why not. No
indeed indeed not.

I hope no one has forgotten the coincidence of Shakespeare's sonnets and Before the Flowers of Friendship Faded Friendship Faded. I hope nobody has. At any rate by the time I am all through and everybody knows not only everything I will tell but everything I can tell and everything I can know then no one not any one will forget will not remember to remember if any one asks any one do they remember, the coincidence between Shakespeare's sonnets and Before the Flowers of Friendship Faded Friendship Faded.

Ordinarily in writing one writes.

Suppose one is writing. It is to be presumed that one knows what it is to be that which one has written.

Suppose one is writing. It is to be presumed that one does not know what it is to be that which they have written.

But in any case one does write it if one is the person who is writing it.

Supposing you are writing anything, you write it.

That is one way of writing and the common way.

There is another way of writing. You write what you intend to write.

That is one way. You write what you intended to write.

There is one way. Is it another way.

You write what has always been intended, by any one, to be written.

Is there another way to write.

You write what some one has intended to write.

This is not an uncommon way of writing.

No one way of writing no way of any of these ways is an uncommon way of writing.

Presumably a great many people write that way.

Now when the same person writes in two different ways that is to say writes as they write, writes as they intended to write, writes as any one intended to write, writes as some one intended to write why does it sound different why does each writing sound different although written by the same person writing. Now why does it sound different. Does it sound different if the words used are the same or are the words used different when the emotion of writing, the intention in writing is different.

That is the funny part of it. That all this is the thing to know. Funny is again used in the sense of diverting and disturbing.

There are then really there are then two different ways of writing.

There is the writing which is being written because the writing and the writer look alike. In this case the words next to each other make a sound. When the same writer writes and the writing and the writer look alike but they do not look alike because they are writing what is going to be written or what has been written then the words next to each other sound different than they did when the writer writes when the writer is writing what he is writing.

The words next to each other actually sound different to the ear that sees them. Make it either sees or hears them. Make it the eyes hear them. Make it either hears or sees them. I say this not to explain but to make it plain.

Anybody knows the difference between explain and make it plain. They sound the same if anybody says they do but they are not the same.

Now another thing. The words next to each other that sound different to the eye that hears them or the ear that sees them, remember this is just to make it plain, do not necessarily sound different to the writer seeing them as he writes them.

We had a motto. This is it.

I am I, not any longer when I see.

There are two different ways in which writing is done is easily done. They are both easy in the same as well as in the different way.

All this begins to make it clear that Shakespeare's plays and Shakespeare's sonnets even when they are all here are different to the eye and ear. Words next to each other are different to the eye and ear and the reason of it is clear. It not only is clear but it will be clear. Words next to each other make a sound to the eye and the ear. With which you hear.

Oh yes with which you do hear.

All this seems simple but it takes a great deal of coincidence to make it plain. A coincidence is necessary all the same to make it plain.

The coincidence happened and then it was plain.

That makes me say that the Before the Flowers of Friendship Faded Friendship Faded had to be written by me before it make it plain, it was for me a coincidence and this coincidence I will explain, I will also tell it to make it plain. I will also tell it so I do tell it just the same.

When I was very young I knew that there was a way of winning by being winsome. Listen to me nevertheless.

Anybody who is a baby or has been one knows this way.

Then later one knows that there is a way of winning by having been winsome.

Perhaps yes nevertheless.

Later one knows there is a way of winning by being intriguing.

Later one knows that there is a way of winning by having been intriguing.

Later every one knows there is a way of winning by simply being able to have them know that you can be displeased by their being displeasing.

Then later there is a way of winning by having been winning.

What has this to do with writing, something and nothing, considerable and everything, a little and very little. But it is useful. It is useful to think of everything if one wishes to reduce anything to two ways. Two ways of any one thing is enough for a beginning and for an ending.

None of these knowledges are knowledges in one way of writing. Any one of these knowledges are knowledges in the other way of writing.

That is to say and this is where everybody who can write and think will say that it is their way, that is to say if you know these things and you can know these things then you can write as if you knew or as if you had known or as if you were going to know these things.

This is an ordinary way of writing and when ordinary writing is written in this way anybody can say that they can read what anybody can say. And if they do do they do it again. Of course they do and that makes them certain of that thing that as they can do it again they have not done it before. Oh yes we all know what to say if we say it that way. Yes yes yes. No one has any need not to guess yes. Or if you like no. What is the difference between no and yes. Think.

On the other hand if you do not know these things although the time will or will not come that you will know these things, then you write as one who has been allowed to know these things without knowing them.

What things. Have you forgotten, because if you have not may be I have. May be I have but I doubt it. May be you have.

The knowledge is that you write what you intend to write because you do or do not win the way you intend to win. Even if you do not win. Or even if nothing. Not even if it is nothing not to be pleasing even if it is nothing to be or not be pleased or to be or not be displeasing. It is not only used as such but it is also only not used as such.

And that makes it all clear just why in the one case and in the other case the words next to each other sound different or not the same.

Is it all clear. Is it all plain.

Or is it why they do not have to say it is not all clear it is not all plain. Forgive no one and partly forgive no one because there is nothing to forgive.

But it is true that there are two ways of writing.

There is the way when you write what you are writing and there is the way when you write what you are going to be writing or what some other one would have written if they had been writing. And in a way this can be a caress. It can not be tenderness. Well well. Of course you can understand and imagine.

And this brings it all to two words next to each other and how when the same person writes what he writes and the same person as that person writes what he is going to write the sound of the words next to each other are different.

The words next to each other can sound different or not the same.

What is a sound.

A sound is two things heard at one and the same time but not together. Let us take any two words.

That is a sound heard by the eyes, that is a sound.

Let us take any two words.

Perhaps he is right even if he seems wrong.

It is all very difficult not to explain nor to know but to do without.

Mr. Owen Young made a mistake, he said the only thing he wished his son to have was the power of clearly expressing his ideas. Not at all. It is not clarity that is desirable but force.

Clarity is of no importance because nobody listens and nobody knows what you mean no matter what you mean, nor how clearly you mean what you mean. But if you have vitality enough of knowing enough of what you mean, somebody and sometime and sometimes a great many will have to realise that you know what you mean and so they will agree that you mean what you know, what you know you mean, which is as near as anybody can come to understanding any one.

Why yes of course, it is needless to say why yes of course when anybody who can say why yes of course can say so.

Now nobody can think, nobody can, that this has nothing to do with Shakespeare's sonnets and Shakespeare's plays, nobody who can, because in no instance is there not a lack of what they have in either one of one.

But they have not the same thing and there is a reason why and a reason why is sound and sense. Oh please be pleased with that. Pleased with what. With very much whatever they have which of course they do have.

Shakespeare's sonnets are not Shakespeare's plays and there is a reason why and they sound different. You all know the reason why and they sound different.

Henry James nobody has forgotten Henry James even if I have but I have not. If Henry James was a general who perhaps would win an army to win a battle he might not know the difference but if he could he would and if he would he might win an army to win not a war but a battle not a battle but an army.

There is no use in denying that there could be a difference can be a difference.

Perhaps, he, make he what you like. If you like or if you do not like whichever you like.

Perhaps he is right even if he seems wrong.

But there is no doubt about seems wrong. There is no occupation in where he went or how he came or whichever or whatever more of which it was like.

Think how you can change your mind concerning this matter.

Think how carefully you can say this.

If you can say this carefully, you can either not change your mind concerning this matter, or you can act entirely differently, that is, you can change your mind concerning this matter.

Remember how Henry James was or was not a general,

And think what there is to express.

All who wish do express what they have to express.

Do you know how every one feels in this world just now. If you do leave it to me to say it again.

I return to the question of the difference between Shakespeare's plays and Shakespeare's sonnets and you do too.

Like it or not if I do you do too and if you do not do it too, you do not do it too.

Do you begin to realise what it is that makes sound.

Think of your ears as eyes. You can even think of your eyes as ears but not so readily perhaps.

Shakespeare wrote plays and in these plays there is prose and poetry and very likely every time one word that makes two words, is next to each other, it makes three sounds, each word makes a sound, that is two words make two sounds and the words next to each other make not only a sound but nearly a sound. This makes it readily that any two words next each other written by any one man make the same sound although all the words and their meaning are different.

That is they do if he feels alike. But there we are that is what it is all about. And what is feeling alike. It is that that makes it important if I say so.

It all depends now here is where it all not commences but is, it all depends upon the two ways to write.

One way is to write as you write, the other way is to write the way you are going to write. And then some can some do once in a while write the way some one would write if they write only they do not that is to say they say they would if they could. That is different than if you think they do that is if you write as if they think they do.

This sounds mixed but it is not and it is so important. Oh dear it is so important.

Before I say which I do say that when Shakespeare wrote his sonnets the words next to each other too but this time they did not make three sounds they made one sound.

There is a reason and this is the reason. I will try you will try. Oh yes you will try, I will try, we will try, if we can we will try to make it all apply. Oh yes we can oh yes we can try, to do this as we do. Yes one of two. One of two ways to write. There are many more but about this no one can or does care because if it makes a difference it does not make a difference too.

So yes. Very well now.

There are two ways to write, listen while I tell it right. So you can know I know.

Two ways to write.

If two ways are two ways which is the only way. Remember how to say a coincidence may occur any day.

And what is a coincidence.

A coincidence is having done so.

Shakespeare he wrote sonnets and Shakespeare he wrote plays but there is no coincidence about that. Not at all. That is an example. Listen. That is an example of the fact that there are two ways of writing. There is the way of writing as it is written those are the plays, and there is the way of writing as it was going to be written and those are the sonnets. Does it make any difference whether the way it was going to be written is his way or some way of somebody's. In this case it does not. That is if you are only interested and just now I am only interested in one of two ways.

But there is a coincidence and that is Before the Flowers of Friendship Faded Friendship Faded. By coincidence I mean just this, this which is that.

The coincidence is simply that. That Before the Flowers was written too in the second way that is as it was going to be written whether as the writer was going or somebody else having been the writer was going to write it. And this makes it be what there is of excitement.

I found out by doing so that when that happened the words next to each other had a different sound and having a different sound they did not have a different sense but they had a different intensity and having a different intensity they did not feel so real and not feeling so real they sounded more smooth and sounding more smooth they sounded not so loud and not sounding so loud they sounded pretty well and sounding pretty well they made everybody tell, just why they like them sounding so well. Oh yes not oh tell. Yes sounding as they sound or sounded very well.

And so I found out that Shakespeare's sonnets were like that and so yes you see it was important to me.

When Shakespeare wrote his sonnets there were words next to each other too but this time they did not make three sounds they made one sound.

And this is why they are different this is why the sonnets are different from the plays and the plays different from the sonnets.

And by a coincidence I found out all about it.

The coincidence was Before the Flowers of Friendship Faded Friendship Faded.

There is no use in hesitating before a coincidence.

Shakespeare's plays and Shakespeare's sonnets are not a coincidence. They are different.

Now it is very entertaining that all this comes out so well between the sonnets because the plays you might say the plays are about what other people did could and would have said, but not at all, not at all at all, they were written while writing not as they were going to be written.

No sound really makes any difference because really a sound is not heard but seen and anything seen is successful.

A thing heard is not necessarily successful.

A thing seen is necessarily successful.

By the time Shakespeare's sonnets have been seen Shakespeare's plays have been heard.

But really this is not true.

Shakespeare's plays have been seen, and any sound seen is successful.

Shakespeare's sonnets have been heard. Any sound heard well any sound heard is heard. Any sound heard if it is heard is successful.

Supposing everybody gets well into their head the difference between the sound seen and heard of Shakespeare's plays and the sound seen and heard of Shakespeare's sonnets and that there is a difference.

Any one can by remembering hear how a thing looks. This sounds foolish but really it is not foolish, it is as easy as anything else.

All natural people say I have heard it burning, I have seen it called, I have heard it shown. They say these things and they are right. One sees much better than one hears sounds.

That is true of all beauty.

You hear the beauty you see the sound.

And so Shakespeare goes on.

And now everybody has a gift for making one sound follow another even when they hesitate.

If they really hesitate then as one word does not follow another there is no such result.

But do they really hesitate. Does any one really hesitate. Or do they really not do this, really and truly not hesitate.

But if they do not hesitate and most people who have a gift of making one word follow another naturally do not hesitate, there is as I have said two ways of writing.

You do understand that about hesitating, there is a waltz called Hesitation, but you do understand that sooner or later than this will then be then about Henry James and his having been a general then and winning a battle then and a war then if there is to be a war then.

But to begin again.

And perhaps again to begin again.

Most people or if they do most people who have a gift of making one word follow another naturally do not hesitate, there is as I have said two ways of writing.

And the two ways are two ways that everybody writes. Some do not ever write the one way or the other way.

Shakespeare did. He wrote both ways.

He wrote as he wrote and he wrote as he was going to write.

One way is the way Shakespeare wrote when he wrote his plays, the other way is the way he wrote when he wrote his sonnets, and the words one after the other next to each other are different in the two different ways.

And now to tell the story of the coincidence.

To have always written in the one way, that is to write so that the writing and the writer not only look alike but are alike, is what has been done by any one, of which one is one.

Remember I wish to say later what Henry James did but that has nothing whatever to do with coincidences, nothing whatever, nothing whatever to do with coincidences.

Those who run can read, I remember as a child being very puzzled by that.

There was a moment many years ago when I had a meaning for it but now I have forgotten that and now I have none.

Supposing it does mean something these words, he who runs can read.

It makes one feel that very likely to feel is to feel well.

If to feel well makes one feel that perhaps it makes one not feel to feel well.

Very likely that is not what they meant, did mean by he who runs can read.

Feel well and add well to feel.

And so he who runs can read.

And that makes partly what they have be theirs.

Oh yes.

If they have partly what they have.

To have written always so that what is it, that what or is written is like that which is doing the writing. If not exactly why not.

To have written always so that which is written is like that that which, who is doing the writing, only, that is, that it not only sounds alike and looks alike but that it is alike.

He who runs can read. I do not know who wrote this line nor what it means but it used to be used in copy books when I went to school.

And this brings us all to Shakespeare's plays and Shakespeare's sonnets and it also brings us to coincidences, and it also brings us to Before the Flowers of Friendship Faded Friendship Faded.

And I often think how Henry James saw.

He saw he could write both ways at once which he did and if he did he did. And there is nothing alike in heard and saw. Not now or ever by itself, not now.

Owen Young said that everything should be clear and everything is now clear.

Or one may say now everything is clear. So much at any rate is clear.

There are the plays and there are the sonnets of Shakespeare and they were written by the same man but they were not written in the same way.

Each lot was written in one of the two ways and the two ways are not the same way.

Henry James and therefore I tell you about Henry James and perhaps being a general and perhaps winning a battle and if perhaps knowing if perhaps winning a war.

The way to find this out all this out is to do likewise, not to do it alike but to do it likewise. Do you see what I mean, how the difference is not the same no not the same which it is not.

The way to find this out find it find it out is to do likewise. That is not to write Shakespeare's plays and Shakespeare's sonnets but to write, write plays and sonnets, and if you do that and I have done that, I have written what I have written and I have written Before the Flowers of Friendship Faded Friendship Faded. Then it comes over you all of a sudden or very slowly or a little at a time why it is all as it is.

You make a diagram or a discovery, which is to discover by a coincidence. Oh yes a diagram I say a diagram to discover by coincidence, that is not what a diagram is but let it be. I say let it be.

You make a discovery, it is a coincidence, of course yes a coincidence, not an accent but an access, yes a coincidence which tells you yes. Yes it makes it possible to make the discovery.

And after that, yes after that, a great deal that has perplexed you about sound in connection with sense is suddenly clear.

Also what the relation of a writer is to his audience, oh yes an audience that is suddenly clear, whether one and one and one makes one or three and just as often one and two, all this all this is clear.

But most of all oh most of all just why two words next to each other make a different sound one way than they do the other way and why oh yes and why.

There is nothing means more than oh yes and why.

I will now patiently tell all about everything.

I had always written myself out in relation to something.

Think everybody think.

Is not that the way all who can run can read.

Perhaps that is what that means. Perhaps there is more to it, there is perhaps the concentration upon the reading as well as upon the running. That is the thing that makes writing.

I have said who has said what has been said whichever I have said or indeed, as it might or might not or even may be left to be said that. And now in or as their fashion.

I have said that there are two ways of writing, writing as it is written writing as it is going to be written whether as the one writing has written or as some one as intended made it for which it is written. If this is so and indeed it is so, then in that case there are the two ways of writing.

Perhaps it is surprising after all after all that I have said that it is the plays of Shakespeare that were written as they were written and the sonnets that were written as they were going to be written.

And in each case I tell you and in each case the words next to each other make a different sound. In one case a smooth sound without which need they mean what they said. In the other case a real sound which need not mean what they said as they just do. Of course they just do.

The sonnets in the sonnets the words next to each other make the smooth sound without which they need to mean what they said.

In the plays they make the lively sound and if they mean what they said they mean it because a lively sound can as it will or if it does mean what is said.

Do you begin to see or do you begin just as well not begin to see.

It is all very interesting curious if one had not found it out by a coincidence but one that is I having found it out by a coincidence it is not curious.

The coincidence as I have said was the writing of Before the Flowers of Friendship Faded Friendship Faded. There too like the Shakespeare sonnets the words next to each other made a smooth sound and the meaning had to be meant as something had been learnt. If not why not.

And in all the other things oh yes in all the other things the words next to each other make a lively sound and they mean which they mean as they mean can they mean as indeed must they mean, I mean. Indeed yes.

And so now anybody can know because I tell them so that the coincidence was so and so and so it was.

Listen to me. And so it was.

Now what has all this to do with Henry James and if he was a general and if he won a battle and if he would be if he would win a war. If he would win a war.

Now Henry James had two ways in one. He had not begun oh dear no he had not begun, he had indeed dear no, not had he begun.

That is one thing.

The other thing is that mostly there are one of two sometimes one of three that do not listen but they hear.

That is what most writing is. Sometimes two of three do listen and do hear.

Perhaps they do if they do it is not queer, it is not queer of them so to do.

Now in the case of Henry James listen in the case of Henry James all of them all three of them listened as if they did or indeed as if they did not hear. Indeed not, indeed they listened as if they did or as if they did listen and not hear or if they all three did listen and did hear. And all of this was not queer not at all not at all queer.

That made it be that Henry James all the same Henry James if he had been a general what would he have done.

I ask you if he had been a general what would he have done.

Let us think carefully about all this.

Then everybody will know that it was not begun.

All that was important to know. For me to know now.

I am carefully going into the question of Henry James.

Before I go any further let everybody think of generals and what they do.

What do generals do.

Of course generals do do something. That is something is done when there are generals. And one general if he is a general does do something. To think of this as Henry James. A general who does do something. What did he do when he did something when Henry James was a general what did he do as he did something which he certainly did.

Henry James is a combination of the two ways of writing and that makes him a general a general who does something. Listen to it.

Does a general or does a general not win a war. Does a general or does a general not win a battle and if he does how does he do it.

Well he does it because not right away or even after a little while nothing happens together and then all of a sudden it all happens together or if not then why not.

Now Henry James if he could not have been otherwise would have had that it was like that. Sometimes not of course sometimes not.

A general can not have it come all at once as often as not if he did then there would be nothing that would happen or if it did nothing would be amiss.

For instance if Henry James had been a general and had not anything to do but this. Of course not he would not then have done have had anything to do but this.

Everything that could happen or not happen would have had a preparation. Oh yes you know you know very well how Henry James had had to do this.

So then if Henry James had been a general what would he have had to have done. This which he did do. Oh yes he would have had to do that which he has done, had done, did do, to do this.

Think anybody think.

How did or does Henry James do this.

He came not to begin but to have begun.

Any general who can win or can not have won a battle has come to do this.

He came not to begin but to have begun.

Henry James came not one by one and not to have won but to have begun.

He came to do this.

Let us think a little how he was this.

He knew why he knew how it would have been begun. Not as beginning but as begun. He knew this not as having been won, not why he knew this and did not know this, never knew this as one, one, one.

Numbers never came or came amiss but it was not whether or not numbers were begun that made him know this.

I like to think of begun. Not as beginning or having begun but as being begun oh yes he could and did with this as this.

Think how Henry James knew which one, which one won. He knew this. That is how a general can win or not win being a general and having or not having won a battle or a war, as this.

It is the same thing.

And Henry James was not the same thing. A general is not the same thing. He was a general, he was the same thing, not the same thing as a general but really one.

Would he lose a battle a battle that was begun. Perhaps yes.

A general which he was could do this.

I like to think how he looked as this which he was when he was one.

I like to think how everything can make one, he was begun, as one.

It is not necessary to know the life history of a general. As I say a battle, as I say a war, a war, a battle is begun, that is what is always happening about it about any one who has been a general and had one had a war had a battle had either one or both of either one.

Let it not make any difference what happened to either one of one.

What did Henry James do, neither he nor I knew. Which is which. It is not necessary to be plainly helped or not. Not at all necessary.

I wish to say that I know that any day it will happen to be the way he knew how Henry James came not to stay not to have gone away but to have begun, oh yes to have begun, that is what I say to have begun, it is necessary, if you are a general, it is necessary, to have begun and Henry James is a general, it is necessary to have begun, which is what has been done.

I like very well what I have said.

Remember that there are two ways of writing and Henry James being a general has selected both, any general has selected both otherwise he is not a general and Henry James is a general and he has selected both. Neither either or or nor.

It was a glorious victory oh yes it was, for which it was, for which oh yes it was.

I can recognise coming to heat hands in winter and plans in summer. But this is not here nor there.

Can you see that any day was no part of his life.

It meant very likely it meant just that, just that is different, as different from only that. In every case they meant as much more as they did.

Oh how can I not recognise that Americans recognise roofs recognise doors recognise theirs recognise cares. Of course they can go where they can go if they go but do they go. If he did.

Henry James was an American, but not as a general as a general he was a European as a general, which he was as he was a European general.

But this may go to make an American if an American which they do can say so.

Henry James never said he never made everything more or nothing more of that. No he did not.

In this way in a little while you will see and really you will see what is American. You will see what is American. If you will see what is American.

If Henry James had been a general which he was what would he have had to do. He would have to do what a general has to do. He would have had to have it begun a battle or a war, if a general is to be a general any more and Henry James was one.

Do not forget that there are two ways to write, you remember two ways to write and that Henry James chose both. Also you must remember that in a battle or a war everything has been prepared which is what has been called begun and then everything happens at once which is what is called done and then a battle or a war is either not or won. Which is as frequently as one, one, one.

You can see that he chose both Henry James, you can see that he was a general Henry James, you can see that a war or a battle may or may not be won or both or one, one, one.

I like Henry James as that.

Volume II

ALL three Jameses sat together. This they naturally would do. Would there be any other Jameses.

In accord with the way that they use what they had and in accord with the hope that they will use what they have all Jameses get together.

After a while all and any James remains or stays apart.

And this cannot be told as they never become old, not any James.

Do generals become old. Yes if they continue to be generals.

So there is a difference between a James and a general, and in a way we come to that.

It makes no difference that they never remember either General or a James.

Nor what they remember that is what they do not remember or rather do not remember. Do you wish a James to remember. Do you wish a general to remember.

Well anyway neither a General nor a James will remember.

And so Henry James is a general.

He has not so many things to do things which he does do but he does do the things which he has to do. Oh yes Henry James does. And that makes it interesting. What he has to do makes it interesting.

That is just like a general is it not just like a general that the thing which he has to do makes it interesting.

All that they have told, no matter whether which it is I wish to refuse that it is told and again refuse that that which it is is told. Oh yes refuse as much as any wish as any anybody which is a wish. Do you see by what I mean that Henry James is not a queen but a general. Oh yes you do you understand that.

Henry James made no one care for plans. Do you see that he is a general. He made nobody care for plans and after all they were fairly able of course they were fairly able.

None of this is what to wish.

Henry James had no wishes and if he were a general he would have no wishes and he was a general and he had no wishes.

In the meantime and there is no intermediate in the mean time Henry James cannot be said to come prepared. Oh yes it seems like that but is it true.

If he had been a general and had to win a war or a battle or even a part of a battle what would he have had to do. He would have done it.

In a way he would have done it. Oh yes in a way he would have won it. I have often thought what he would do if he had been a general.

Volume III

I LIKE to think what would he do if he had been a general.

Volume IV

LITTLE by little he would have been a general but would he have been a general little by little. Not at all. He would not have been a general little by little. He would have been begun as a general. That is what he would have been begun, he would have been begun a general.

And after a little while the three Jameses would again have sat together. Just as they did. Having sat together. And would there have been any other Jameses. Just as well any other Jameses as there often are. Even to be said habitually are.

And when any three Jameses sat together you might say they sat in a circle as they sat together as three Jameses sat together any of them would have been what they were. Would Henry James have been a general. Why not. I see no reason why not.

I can again think how they sat if they sat.

But they did sit.

Henry James did sit and as he sat the way he sat was the way he would have sat if he had been a general and so there we are, or at least yes there we are.

Now do you understand what I mean by what I say and what he was and what he was in what there is to be what he was. He was a general because a general is begun. He was a general because he sat as one who had been and was still the general he had been.

Three Jameses sat together but that did not make any difference. That might happen or might have happened or indeed did happen does happen to any general who has and still has been a general.

I wish to disclose everything I know.

I wish to disclose why I feel a general so.

He felt a general can feel that he need never kneel.

What do I mean to say. That he was not married in any way. And is that true as a general or is it true in general. No it is not true in general but he as a general of him it is true as a general.

And why not.

Once more if not why not.

Because if alike allowed alike, he would catch it all as they say. This to him was not more important than if he wished either not to be there or to be alone.

Now I wish to say generously why he was never married either as a general or as a man.

How can a man be a general too. Not if no one knew.

But he knew.

He knew that he was a general too.

And now yes so you do.

How was he a general.

Not by not being married or yes is it as nice.

He was a general by the circumstance that he had begun and if a general has been married it is of no importance.

How when Henry James was a general did he conduct his war. There is no difference between conduct and how did he conduct his war.

Did he win his battle or did he win his part of his battle if he was not the full general or the only general in his battle. If he did not, but he did, why not.

There are two things to be said. He was not married, to be said and he was a general, to be said.

He was not married not only for this reason but of which he did not take part.

He took part in the battle, which is the battle in which he as a general did take his part. And if the battle which was the battle in which he did take his part was won then as a general he did take part in winning the battle which was won. Also the war.

Thank you, also the war.

How can you state what you wish to say. That is the question. What you wish. That is the question. To say. That is the question.

By being called to kindle.

What do you wish to say.

When Henry James was this general which he was and they made the most of that, by the time they did, and he was not married, which he undoubtedly was not, and placed beside, where they had the right, whenever it happened, and they on their account, made mention of their violence by any failure, no more than of course told in toiling, so they could undoubtedly in time, face themselves there, where.

It is not only in this and in this way that a battle is fought.

It is of great importance that Henry James never was married.

That might make theirs be mine.

Volume V

FOR which they spare neither one of themselves. No general that is a general as a general has won one at a time.

Believe me if you like.

Volume VI

I THINK easily of three who sat and one who did that.

Volume VII

I, HE, it may not be set in place of stated.

I state that it may not be settled in place of stated.

He may not be seated to settle in place of stating what there is to be stated.

It may not be of advantage to have no settlement in place of not stating what is to be settled in place of settling.

In this way he could adventure to wander away from being a general. But in every little while more may be there.

This is the way it was with Henry James.

And so what is there to say.

If he had been a general what would he have had to do, he would have had to take part in a battle if there was a battle in a war if there were a war if not then why not.

But no questions can be asked to which no questions can have as an answer.

And so they make an occasion of this.

This makes you see how lightly or heavily a general can take place.

May they recognise being married as yes and no in marriage.

Henry James had no marriage as he was not married. They were obliged to give this answer. Not when they heard him. Or even after they had him.

So often do generals but generals are not more than are more.

That makes a general no hazard.

A general begun.

Why can marriage be made away.

Henry James was not married. By this they mean what they say.

I wish to tell you all who wish to hear why marriage married if they can name him here.

They do name him.

They name him Henry James.

A little still a little by that they all grew.

For which I ask you, how do you do.

Volume VIII

To COME back to that he never was married would he be very likely to live alone and if he was very likely to live alone would he be as if he were alone. Now think of any general any regular general and how it would be.

If he were not married and lived alone he would live as if he were not married and lived alone but really not he would live as if he were not married. If they are not married do they live as if they live alone. Think about this a Henry James and think about this a general and then think about this as this.

What did he make him do when he wrote what did it make him do when he had it to do to help with a battle or help with a war or help with whatever he ordered that he should help. He would of course never help himself. Any one who is not married and who lives as if he is not married does not help himself. He can not help himself. And this makes him write as he does, does or was.

In many instances marriages are arranged in many instances of generals. Was Henry James one of such a one. In a way not because he was not married and if he was not married it was not because he was ever married. No not for instance not one.

A great deal has to do with everything. And marrying.

Well will they lightly go away.

For which they knew who likes a crowd. Or who will please when they lower or do not lower a boat.

He was or was not prepared for as much as he had.

This has nothing or something to do with either not married or not.

Believe those who do not rather not have to leave it as that.

He never felt awkward as married but he should recite only really who could or did recite or not quite.

I tell you and it is a fact if you are not married why are you married or not. Henry James or a general were never like that.

And that after all is not all or everything they have to say.

The thing to wonder is did he not have to say what he did not have to say.

That can happen to any general who is regularly a general.

Any general.

Volume IX

Now who has or wills to have that they have or have to have and whether, whether will they have or rather.

I could count many times as many wives and Henry James or a general could not count as many times as many wives and what difference does that make if they venture or do not place a general before or after. A general is placed before or after and so is Henry James. He is placed before or after.

And no doubt a married no doubt a married man is not no doubt a married man is doubt.

Henry James or a general are never in tears about a married man and so they are not.

What could they feel if they live.

They could if they could feel if they live they could feel or they could live or they could do both or they could not and if not if they did not is did not the same as could not or if indeed if could not is not the same who will change the same.

Henry James meant and met and if he was a general and he was if he was a general and if is not necessary because he was he was not ready but being not ready was of no importance because he was.

I wish to say he was.

Rather I wish to say he was.

I wish rather to say he was.

I wish now to give the life history of Henry James who was a general. And yes. Whether no or yes whether yes or no or to tell it so.

I wish not wish but do do tell it so.

There is no hope of either or oh no.

Volume X

Henry James may be, not a place he could not be a place a general cannot be a place, he or it can not.

Henry James then can not be a place and in so much as he is not a place and can not be a place and a general can not be a place and is not a place insomuch Henry James is a general and a general is Henry James.

Oh yes they say there can be others but oh yes there are not.

Henry James begins to be as he is. Indeed if not why not. But there is never any if not as Henry James is as he is. He controls nothing by only that but a general a general controls nothing oh no oh yes a general controls something, and so triumphantly I say triumphantly and so triumphantly so does Henry James he controls something he does control something. And so when and why not is not Henry James a general and a general Henry James. They are that. Henry James is a general and he controls something even though and it can be said that Henry James does not control anything and even then it can be said a general does not control anything.

Who has a general at heart or Henry James. They have that with that wish.

Pray pray pray prepare to wish.

Henry James comes for them for them and them.

Was a general known to wish.

No no general not as a general a general was not known to wish.

Neither was Henry James.

Volume XI

THERE is no use always beginning before before what. I wished to say wish to say that there is no use there is no use in my beginning in my having been beginning before. Once more I have it to do before what. Before he was Henry James. Before he was a general. Some one might they be some one. Not before. Not before Henry James. Might he be some one before Henry James. Not if he was to have been Henry James which he was and a blessing even if not everything a blessing something not to be arranging to be Henry James. A general is in any and all of any way or ways the same.

But to begin. Having begun there is no refusal in to begin but there might be. In this case there might only be as there more than just there there might have been.

Think of an American thing a poetic American thing there might have been.

This may not refer to a general. Not may but also not might, might not refer to a general. May or might not refer to Henry James. All of which connects with not to begin. In a new continent and is any new continent, no not new, in a new continent they might not begin not might not have been begun. That makes a new continent not any fun.

Why do you say so if you know so.

Henry James might not have begun. Neither a general too.

I wish to think a little of a difference in age and why nobody says so. And is there any hope of sitting there or any where. Or is there any hope of using any hope.

I wish to see that you know Henry James.

I may be acquainted with him by and by.

Who says it is easily said. Who says or said that it was easily said.

Forget who said what was easily said and come back to remember Henry James.

One at a time is of no use as just as often there is more than not one at a time. In place of that who is in place of that.

This makes partly an understanding of Henry James and I am not as pleased as not relieved that it is so.

One should always think well of how to spell.

All who have have it to do so.

As newly as not wed Henry James.

For this and made for this as in and for a use a use for this.

Of and for are always different and never no never different as not one at a time.

I begin to see how I can quiver and not quiver at like and alike.

A great deal can be felt so.

Volume XII

HENRY JAMES one.

Volume XIII

THE young James a young James was a young James a James. He might be and he might be even might be Henry James.

Volume XIV

ONCE upon a time there was no dog if there had been a dog nobody wept.

Once upon a time there was no name and if any one had a name nobody could cover a name with a name. But nobody except somebody who had not that name wept.

Once upon a time there was a place for a name and when that name was the same no one and why not if no one, no one wept. Once upon a time if once upon a time a name was not to blame not to blame not if as a name, if once upon a time a name was the same and if not no one had any one to blame then no one not this time no one had to weep and so this time and no one at this time had been having it as a blame that no one was weeping as if no one had wept.

Once upon a time no one not any one wept that there was a name which was the same as the same name. And so no one wept.

Volume XV

ONCE upon a time if you wonder once upon a time what was his name, his name Henry James was a name, and weeping he wept.

If he wept was it his name.

Oh yes it was his name, all the same yes all the same it was his name. He wept.

Volume XVI

ANY time Henry James wept it was his name.

Volume XVII

To RETURN but nobody can, if they can may they if they began, to return to Henry James.

Not to say this slowly is not to say this not at all. To say this not at all slowly is not not to say this at all.

And so all.

All can return slowly.

Nobody can return slowly if they do not move. And did they move. If they did not better than if they did which they did move.

Henry James cannot return slowly. Or have it as a pleasant and a pleasure. Pleasant in time.

How can all who have arranged to remain where or when or wherever may they may they be alike.

Nobody is alike Henry James.

Better prepare enough.

Nobody is alike Henry James.

Is it is that it, is it because Henry and James are both first names.

Believe this if this is true.

Does it mean that you are you or who are you.

Henry James and names.

He neither now or either how invented names.

May be by a character. Or may be or may be not.

Nobody could make a mistake.

If for instance nobody could make a mistake.

I wish I was used to think of a difference between won and young.
Which made around around.
He heard nobody care.
But this was this or is it.
He he who heard nobody care.
Or is or is it.
He or he and he was prepared to remain there.
Not exactly not.
He was not not prepared not to remain where, there where.
In his care.
In its care.
Where.

It is delightful to know who can go home if they go and if they do not if they do not go.

I have to say here here I very well know what it is that has happened.

He will not begin again because he has it is has been begun.

I have said it for me there.

Which will undertake that care.

I understand you undertake to overthrow my undertaking.

Henry James when he was young.

We discussed we said we discussed did or was he young.

She said he was fresh that is fresher but he was not young and I said he was young quite young that is what I said.

And he was not young but fresher then or was he young and not fresher then.

Which one went on, one not before the other one.

If they were not the same.

If he were young that is to say had been he would have been read to been a young or younger one. I think this is a thing.

Not only by a wish but by not watches or wishes.

He had both both watches and wishes Henry James when he was fresher or Henry James when he was young.

There is no use hanging on to some one wishes and watches but some have some hung when that is young that one.

Decline may make or makes one at a time.

There is no decline when they are not sickly when they are young.

That is one thing.

Henry James one thing.

Henry James for one thing.

He never pursued one at a time no not one thing a thing.

That was not one thing a young thing but he was a he was a young thing. Henry James was was was a young thing. If he was fresher then fresher and add her. But not by him. Not any one thing.

I wish to add that I knew I know one thing.

One thing one thing.

That Henry James was young one thing.

Prepare for flight.

Henry James did not prepare for flight.

Hours what. What are hours for. Hours are not for one thing.

Anything makes nothing and nothing makes anything not a young thing.

Any one is easily equal to that.

Forgive wishes with watches nor watches with wishes.

Forget one thing.

This makes it feel reasonable not to read but indeed this one thing that Henry James was young with one thing.

For them for names for days.

Not which had been. He had not been. That makes him a young then a middle aged thing not so fresh a thing that he had not been. Which he had not been.

But all the same it is true he had been a young thing.

It is not difficult not very difficult to remember what he had been, any one can any day in walking see anything. Anything is any one and any one is a young one. Oh yes you do. He did too.

When this was true where were they. They were here. He was here. This that was so. He was here where he would have been to have been told that it was so.

Henry James you see Henry James was young. Not necessarily but nicely young. Is there any difference between necessarily and nicely. Not when one had been begun.

And then he went on as if he had been young. Oh yes he did go on as if he had been young. No doubt about it yes this was the way it was when he had been begun.

Henry James never came amiss. He did not come slowly nor did he come to kiss.

Which may be there which may be there which may be there.

Did no one not run.

Added bliss to miss and miss to kiss and kiss to remember remember any one.

This made him be have been young.

So I say it is not only not that he was freshened and had been begun but that he had been young.

There now add nothing whatsoever as to how it never meant more than allow.

I wish every one knew exactly how to feel, about Henry James.

Volume XVIII

I MAY remember how to walk up and down.

Volume XIX

THEY felt as well as very well and in no sort and at no time, well very nearly addedly as well.

This makes that they fell which and where they kneel.

Henry James had well you might say he had no time.

Volume XX

BUT just as much as it might be that he was uneasy not uneasy not afraid.

They might be caught alone. Who might be caught alone.

Volume XXI

THERE might not only be left as it.

As it is a chance to bequeathe.

He felt as if they met with which they met not to bequeathe which in their change they met.

How could Henry James fancy that with his name it was not a similar name to that of his brother. Was his brother another.

There now you see. It is not necessary never to mention never to have a brother.

Fortunately many foil an instance of that.

She bowed to her brother.

That is coming in here.

Volume XXII

I WISH to make it perfectly clear that this is neither there nor here.

Henry James is adamant if you say so.

Volume XXIII

BY WHICH he may and did mean if you say so.

Volume XXIV

LET me tell the history of Henry James simply tell the history of Henry James which brings me and us back to names.

I still have nothing to say about names even if I make a mistake.

Volume XXV

A NAME is a name by which some one reads something or if not then why does he does she not.

And if he does if she does, does it make a moon.

A moon is no name.

James is no name

Henry is no name.

Why is no name.

Shares is no name.

Blinded is no name

Predicate is no name.

This is no name.

Henry James if you say so Henry James was a name.

You can think of a name as a name or not a name. It is very easy to think of Henry James as not a name.

When a boy is a general that is to be is going to be a general being the son and the grandson of one and another one and either of them have been a general they may say to him you cannot be afraid. And he may say but I am I am afraid, I am often afraid, I am afraid when I see something and it turns out to be a horse then I am afraid. But then how can you come to be a general. But a general is on a horse and on a horse it is not on a horse that there is any way to be afraid. And beside that any general is not where it is any danger to be a general in any danger as a general oh no not indeed not for a general. So that is it.

Henry James if he was to be a boy was then to be a general oh yes if not then if not why not a general. But he is and was to be a general.

Come often to see me is not said by a general.

But any one can see a general indeed yes any one.

Henry James was a general.

In general.

The general likes his coffee cold.

In general.

He does not take coffee or milk. Not in general. Not at all. Not a general.

That may be a general.

But Henry James is a general.

And now read what he says.

What does a general say when they read what he says.

In general.

To come back to having been a boy.

Is there a difference between having been a boy and being begun. Not at once and at the same time.

But it is true.

Henry James has been a boy, and he has been begun.

He was never so otherwise.

No never so otherwise.

And this is what is painful that when in tears he was never so otherwise.

But when in tears was he so otherwise.

A general was a general so.

If the little boy was afraid there were no tears because if he was to be a general it would be so otherwise.

When once when twice when once when twice there were no tears otherwise than no tears not twice not once not otherwise.

And so after all anybody can see after all that Henry James was after all a general.

Volume XXVI

PLAY to remember everything that happened within to him.

But which was otherwise when they were not happening.

Play be otherwise.

Can a general be otherwise.

Can he play be otherwise.

Can he play happened to him.

When they happened to him did they happen within.

Did they happen otherwise than it happened for him.

Not otherwise.

Henry James was very ready to have it happen for him.

Volume XXVII

A NARRATIVE of Henry James told by one who listened to some one else telling about some one entirely different from Henry James.

To some one entirely different from Henry James is a woman who might have killed somebody else another woman only very probably she did not. She was not really under any suspicion of having killed her or any other woman or any other man but really she was entirely a different kind of human being from Henry James entirely a different kind of human being and one who had led and did lead an entirely different kind of life. She lived alone and in the country and so did Henry James. She was heavy set and seductive and so was Henry James. She was slow in movement and light in speech and could change her speech without changing her words so that at one time her speech was delicate and witty and at another time slow and troubling and so was that of Henry James. She was not at all at all at all resembling to Henry James and never knew him and never heard of him and was of another nationality and lived in another country. And that is all there is to it.

So one has quite frequently told different people about her. Because it is a matter that remains to be told about her that something is what any one can tell about her.

Indeed very often as often as ever and yet again and once more as often.

So that is why I like to listen to her to the one that tells any story that she tells about what happens to any one and something did happen at least it happened near that one.

This one the one telling the story had always admired Henry James. So there you are. That is the connection.

Volume XXVIII

HENRY JAMES fairly well Henry James.

Volume XXIX

IT MAKES no difference what you say when you read.

It makes no difference what you say if you read.

Neither does it make any difference what you say because you read. None of this makes any difference.

Now think about what does or does not make any difference.

Think about it and do not cry although tears do come easily at least they seem to come easily if they come or if they do not come.

Now when what you say does not make any difference and tears do or do not come and if they do come or if they do not come they could come easily or not easily in coming or not coming this is what it is when Henry James gradually one can not say gradually because by that time it was there but gradually what it was that was said came to rise not like cries but like tears and no one can say that they did or did not come easily but one might say indeed and could say that they did or did not come at all and this made it all there.

Now do you see what I mean when I read.

Even if I do not read do you see what I mean if I do read.

That is what Henry James did, any one does but all the same he did it like that.

Shall I tell you again all about tears and how they rise and how they come and how they will and how they can or not be full. Full is a word so well-known.

Who knows who is well-known.

Henry James is well-known.

But of course he is Henry James is well-known.

Sometimes I wonder about a name like James when it is not a first name but when it is a last name.

David James.

Henry James could not have been named David James.

There was a wicked family named James, and their names make James a very different name and no one needs to feel that tears could come to mean that as a name.

Henry James. A very different name from David James or William James or Robin James or Winslow James. Or even a very different name from Ethel James although that is not so far away, Ethel James and Henry James. Thomas James can never harden any one to the name James. But nevertheless in no distress Henry James is well-known.

Volume XXX

To COMMENCE to cover the ground.

Volume XXXI

It WILL soon be thought that anybody can be bought.

It will not soon be thought that anybody can be taught.

What can anybody buy.

Anybody can buy, that anybody can cry.

Henry James moved as he bought.

There are other words that no one need use, caught, fought taught.

Henry James was meant by all.

Has any country forgot any country.

That is what they try to say.

But what do they say.

That is what there is. What do they say.

For which five mean as six.

Volume XXXII

I AM going to tell it very well.

Volume XXXIII

HE KNEW what was in a name all the same.

Volume XXXIV

IT HAS been remarked and it is very curious that in opening a page you know it is that page not by its age not by the words upon the page not by the number upon the page but because on that page there are three names and those three names are not together upon any other of any page.

Now this has been told to me and is it true. If it has been told to me it certainly is true.

Further more it has been told to me that very likely nothing is said upon that page about any one whose name is upon that page. This has been told to me and it is true it is true that it has been told to me.

And in this way you see that everything that has been told to me is true if it has been told to me.

Henry James is well-known as that oh yes as that.

And now consider fortune and misfortune failure and success, butter and water, ham and water cress.

First then fortune and misfortune. He had no fortune and misfortune and nevertheless he had no distress and no relief from any pang. Any pang. Oh yes any pang.

And failure and success. He had no failure and no success and he had no relief from any failure and he had no relief from any distress. Nevertheless. He had no relief not as having had a relief from any other pleasure and anxiety and in that place any removal and any surprise.

This what has been arranged to say has not been said but all that I have heard has been said. Which they may say. Has been said.

Once upon a time nobody managed to be useful and nobody managed to be there.

Once upon a time and tears will flow once upon a time nobody has arranged to be useful and nobody has arranged as yet and further yet not anybody need have been placed to arrange that anybody wept. In place is not the same as in spite of all. And yet well-known is not more easily arranged. In place of that not well-known is not more than more easily arranged.

I wish to help myself to as much as they had more.

That is what they said not to me but not that is not not to me.

And so it happened I wish you to know to know it as often as well as not very-well that is is not not to me.

What they said to me they said as if it were true and what is there to say.

Some do some do tell some do say so, as if it were so. Some some do. Some do do so.

Some do.

Some do not.

But some who do not say so do not say so. They say some do say that some some one does or do. Do what there is or is not to do. Some do.

GEORGE WASHINGTON

SCENERY AND GEORGE WASHINGTON

A NOVEL OR A PLAY

Characters

Page 1

SCENERY may be autumn scenery.

George Washington is mentioned. He is also remembered.

Autumn scenery is warm if the fog has lifted.

And the moon has set in the day-time in what may be drifting clouds. It sets very quickly and this is when, any one is watching and it is setting in the day-time when the sun is shining. Any sign is a good sign.

Page 2

SCENERY if seen makes a home a home of their seeing how happily she may choose flowers. Will she feed him. George Washington is a memory he may be welcome. Not indeed with theirs as he may be welcome. Scenery if in the autumn is beautiful and very resembling and we are content to have it.

What is scenery. Scenery is a pleasure. And they might say they have not forgotten.

Nor if they are happy with the scenery they might say that scenery is their amount and they may nor will it be that it is not forgotten. For them or for themselves. In autumn.

Page 3

IN AUTUMN there are birds singing in some trees. The scenery in autumn is lovely.

The George Washington is not a memory.

He has been in the country.

Autumn scenery is lovely and as it is a good season and there is little money it is easy to find men workers.

George Washington was the father of his country. He was first in war first in peace and first in the hearts of his countrymen his life is not a memory.

The scenery of autumn is very lovely. There are many walnuts and the marshes are not empty nor are the rocks of trees nor of their color nor is there any lack of plenty.

Page 4

SHE may prefer flowers to scenery roses to rivers dahlias to pleasures and daisies to their place. It is very often lovely to see scenery. Autumn scenery may be like summer that is as to climate.

George Washington spelled alike and born in February. All who will love to peal nuts and even not mean to leave any one or rather in the autumn seeing nuts lie will stoop and get them or else not may be said to be resembling to George Washington in respect to their birthday being in the month of February.

If it rains it spoils the autumn scenery because it causes the leaves to fall.

Poplars in fours not an autumn landscape fours of poplars not an autumn landscape fours in poplars not autumn scenery. A dog does what he should.

They will come to be ready to find autumn warm it may be it may very well be warm in autumn.

George Washington may be easy to write.

Page 5

To FIND autumn scenery. They will see it readily. They will admire it and it is agreeable find it agreeable when it is warm.

George Washington.

Weigh feathers. This makes autumn scenery and it is very beautiful. As well be happy.

George Washington was and is the father of his country.
No not by themselves they will be unknown.
Autumn scenery is beautiful and it is regularly satisfied as an occasion.
They will occasionally visit me.

Page 6

AUTUMN or scenery brothers close or well. Will they care for the color.
Which they make of the vine. Because it is very well if it must matter.

In autumn it is very warm.

And therefore they will please those who say the others told him how
soon in the day. At day break he saw her and he went toward her and
she was well on her way. Any day earlier any day. On an autumn day.
It is dangerous. Because they might be there. They always are because
it is the place for them to be.

But to her. Did it. Any autumn day is different from any summer
day or any winter day.

George Washington is pleased to come that is all who are ready are
ready to rule.

Page 7

PLEASE do not let me wander.

Page 8

SHE is very sleepy. George Washington.

She is very sleepy. The autumn scenery when seen at a distance need
not necessarily be tempted by wind. They may clear skies. But not a
new moon. In autumn a new moon is well advanced. And a cloud can
never cover it partly or be gracious rather to like red and blue all out
but you. George Washington is famous as a nation.

Page 9

SHE may be dark it may be dark and as well. He colors with pleasure
as well.

The autumn landscape is warmer with a full moon.

It should not be a disturbance if they can mistake a bird for a bat or a bat for a bird and find it friendly.

They may be three to sing severally that George Washington may be seen to be beautifully with when they dwell then upon the beauty and autumn beauty of autumn scenery. One in two and one in three and one in one. And they may be not with some which may be that they are better with me. One and one. Or may be made a sum.

Page 10

AUTUMN scenery can be called summer.

It can also be dry and rain.

It need be only when they are and were well and happy. They may include their reception.

It is not part of the time that it is an advantage.

What is autumn landscape they cannot plough.

What also is autumn landscape since as because they can collect all that is grown.

What do they like in autumn landscape after a while they like it to turn into rain.

George Washington may easily have come and gone also have gone also have come. And so they think it very welcome.

So much of it turning rapidly from trimming to feeling and from feeling to varying.

May they be thankful. In case of which pleases. An autumn landscape pleases. And there is sun.

Page 11

IF IT rains will it stop if it rains will it go on in autumn.

Each one of twenty men and twenty women each one of any men or any women may be in place of men and women. And so be ready. Are you ready yet. Not yet.

It is very often thoughtless to ask for more than they are needing.

And in such a way if it is raining in autumn it is easy to wait for rose planting and also to ask a favor. Will they grant. Very likely.

There is warm rain in autumn and cold wind and a large sun and a moon easily not seen as coming and as staying. They may be very likely as well to satisfy and particularly at a distance.

What could be done at noon can be done at night.

They will think very well of having some rain again. George Washington is often broken. As very well.

•

Page 12

PUT you where they can.

When they see they may.

Or they will.

Autumn is made of they well and willing to go about at night when the weather is warm and when the weather is cold when it is wet and a pleasure to them as they may be easily in and out.

Autumn scenery is not made of dahlias.

Autumn scenery either.

Autumn scenery is not made of dahlias nor of whether they gather dahlias.

Autumn scenery may be nicely when the weather is warm and the snow not cold autumn scenery may be nicely when they can and the autumn scenery is autumn scenery in September to January. For which they may be going to thank. And so George Washington is meant to be peopled.

A play and an event.

Also a story and their birth.

Possibly the men and their arrival.

May be they will.

Page 13

OUGHT fourteen to be very well when they will be thirteen. And so they understand distress in the country districts which they have not there not in the. Country districts.

Page 14

ALL call exuberance or all call or all sigh with pleasure that they enjoy their exuberance in not alone not only made in theirs and with enjoy.

An autumn scenery may be debated. They may claim rich and poor in moon and mist and very clearly a lit house. Or other may they order or in a claim refuse a house made a name.

Autumn scenery they call autumn scenery.

She may relish autumn scenery.

Nor will they place autumn scenery unaware.

Should for them declare. They declare. Nor indeed. In choice.

Autumn scenery has hope of a welfare in summer. Or where.

Autumn scenery she feels nicely.

Why is George Washington ought.

Pleasure in alike autumn scenery.

OR A HISTORY OF THE UNITED STATES OF AMERICA

HE ASKED me to tell him why he loved me so and the reason was clearly this that the United States of America is a nation.

What is the United States of America. It is a country of a great size in the center of which there is a great deal of land. Upon this land live those who can do and do whatever they have to do. He asked him to do what they did.

Let me tell about the character of the people of the United States of America and what they say.

Let me tell you one thing, what they say has a great deal to do with what they do, and what they do they do do, as what they were was part of what they did, as by the time, this time, they are what they are.

How do they know what they are. They know it by looking at what they do. This is why the United States of America is important.

Let me tell just what I tell anybody and everybody.

George Washington as well.

I could avoid mentioning what I think of the name of George and just again, well just again, it has happened just again there it is just again, more than other five named George there is another one and his name is George Hawkins.

What is the difference between George Washington and George Hawkins. There is no difference because I think I see George Washington, he was first in peace first in war and first in the hearts of his country men and what would he have done if he had written. Why he would have written them. And so there is a difference between George Washington and George Hawkins or any five of them, the five Georges and everything. So then.

I could never think I liked to look into a place where the windows not being shuttered one can see them eating and being through eating one of them and that one a young woman is standing and talking, that is reading. She stands by the table and the rest of them are all still sitting. It seems a pleasant scene and they are not scarce not scarce nowadays.

That is to say pleasant scenes such as this I have just been describing are not scarce nowadays.

I can say what I have to say. George Washington did not write a play. He wrote at a novel every day. He who was the father of his country.

I wish to say all I think about pleasant scenes which are not scarce nowadays.

George Washington was fairly famous because he wrote what he saw and he saw what he said. And this is what I do. And so what do I do. I say he wrote what he said he did. And he did do what he saw he did. Oh yes he did.

Believe me it was a nice novel the novel that he wrote.

In the first place what has happened. This has happened that nowadays if pleasant scenes were scarce there would be nothing to do because since the excitement of doing or not doing anything is over there naturally must be a recourse to pleasant scenes.

There can be pleasant scenes even in an army if it is fighting but that is of no importance not now at any rate when they are not fighting. When they are fighting pleasant scenes are not only pleasant but only as pleasant, not as pleasant.

Listen to me while I tell what you are all willing to hear.

Pleasant scenes are pleasant and they are not necessarily made to be left. Indeed quite the contrary.

George Washington. George Washington loans. He does not loan incidents because he neither loans nor wishes for incidents. He tells well he tells.

Even why they like it is one of the reasons.

Let me break through and hear them looking. At a pleasant scene which is one of as many pleasant ones.

George Washington may be careful when he starts in to write one. One one one, they make not three or two or one. One one one is the way to keep one from being any other one. And so George Washington was one and he did one and he wrote one and this if he wrote one was the one.

No one had need of one, or one and one, or if not one one one.

To come back to the history of the United States of America a subject about which I am quite fond of talking.

And I am fond of talking about Napoleon but that has nothing to do with novel writing. Napoleon could not write a novel, not he. Washington could. And did. Oh yes I say so. And did.

That has been quite frequently described pleasantly and I am going to do it again. Oh yes again.

Three pleasant people talking about America. I will not mention their names because they have been discovered.

George Washington is not one name George Wickham is not one name Joseph Jones is not one name. And yet oh yes and yet George Washington is a name.

How often do I ask once before how much more there is than one name. Often and often and once more how much more is there than one name.

George Washington is a name a pleasant name and all the same it is a name.

And what did he do.

Everybody knows what he did and what he did not do.

But does everybody know that he wrote novels too. I wonder. I wonder if everybody knows that. But they will. They will because I will tell them the way that he did that.

What is the United States of America.

It is not a country surrounded by a wall or not as well by an ocean. In short the United States of America is not surrounded.

He knew.

He knew that.

And what was the result of his knowing that.

The result of his knowing that was that he said this and in saying this he began a novel, the novel the great American novel. Oh yes he did.

By this I mean all this.

Listen quietly.

The United States of America is not where it is as other countries are. It is there as they say and they held it right there. Held or hold it right there. They themselves held it right there. And this is the history of not only but also the people of the United States of America. And what did they do. What did they if they do say this of this.

George Washington made no mistake. He made no mistake in writing anything or more than anything which he did. He did not make that a mistake.

What did he do.

He wrote a novel.

And not only one but more.

And what kind of a novel did he write.

He wrote several novels some of the same kind and some of different kinds.

He wrote historical novels and natural novels and artificial novels.

And he prepared novels.

And he concluded novels.

And he wished for novels.

Of course he did anybody can and does wish for novels.

Nevertheless.

I say that pleasantly is not presently but just now.

He wished for novels.

Everybody knows his life.

He knew his life and he wished for novels. And he did not confine himself to wishing for novels he wrote novels. He certainly did.

Any one whom I convince is convinced of this.

Think well while I tell you what the people of the United States are.

Volume I

Do THEY know what a novel is.

This has been said by some one to some one and it was meant as a reproach. Do you know what a novel is.

The history of the United States of America. I have often said that. I will say this. I do say this now listen to this.

He was born in the country back of Pittsburg Penn. He enlisted in the American army. He went with the army that is he went in the army to San Antonio Texas on the border of Mexico.

After the United States of America came into the great war that is into the world war that is the war of 1914 to 1918 he came to Europe in the army but in civilian clothes. He was in the intelligence department.

After the four years in the army the war was over and he took his discharge in St Nazaire.

He had the money from his trip back from St Nazaire France to San Antonio Texas he had most of his pay coming to him and he had a little sum of money beside. Francs were then around 35 to a dollar and he changed it all into francs.

He lived with a frenchman who had a place which his family had had for four hundred years and this frenchman knew all about his family right back to the crusades.

He grew all sorts of things to sell all sorts of things that he could grow on this place the American did. He grew a hundred pigeons and rabbits and then he was in constant communication with the people who sell seeds and he did what they told him and once he grew a cabbage of a kind that is usually small and it filled his whole wheel-barrow. This he did by digging up the ground and letting it lie for ten days and then he put in something into the ground something that they sent him and then he planted and had as a result the big cabbage. He did everything the seed people told him and he telephoned to them all the time and whenever the weather changed. All this cost a great deal of money.

He and the frenchman lived like that. Whatever he had the frenchman could have and whatever the frenchman had he the American could have. Then the frenchman's wife died and the frenchman went crazy. He had to be locked up.

There was no way to prove that the American had ever had any money. He had twelve thousand francs left and he used half of it that is six thousand francs to prove that he had had money but he did not get it proved. The brothers of the frenchman did not have much money. The American had always helped in the house when visitors who were the same kind as the frenchman came to the house to visit.

The American went to Bordeaux and there he became a ship's carpenter. He sooner or later married a Bretonne from the Loire Inferieure who had a baby face and was later twenty-six years old. She was small and she could cook but she did not like to because when she did she could not eat and when she was hungry she would go to any restaurant where something looked good to eat to her and eat it.

They found Bordeaux a dead place and came to Paris.

During this time they had a baby. The baby was born in a french place and it was alright a nice little girl and it drank a lot of milk.

When it was twenty-nine days old it looked kind of sick so the mother took it to the nearest baby place and the doctor said how much milk have you been giving it. The mother told him, cut it down by half said the doctor. They did.

In a day or two the baby looked worse and so they took it not to a baby doctor but to a real doctor. He was nice and said I think your baby is not very well I think it is sick, you had better take it back where it was born.

It was Saturday night and they were in a hotel but late that night the American said we better take her anyhow. They got into a taxi and took the baby. The doctor when he saw them was very nice. He looked at the baby and he said I guess the baby is not very well I guess it is pretty sick and he was right because in two days it was dead.

The American had a few thousand francs but he wanted a job, one day a princess came to the legion and said that she wanted a valet. Somebody at the legion suggested the American. He went and his wife went sometimes although she was now going to have another baby and did not much want to cook, so the princess found an english man to cook, a big good looking Englishman but he did not like to cook either. They also had a finnish ladies maid and she could because the house was so full of mirrors be seen reflected somewhere any time listening to what was going on. The American had not gotten another job because the Bretonne said that she is going to keep the baby, a child should know its mother, she said. Perhaps she might cook.

What is the difference between all this and a novel.

Ah yes. But there is not any.

But there is.

And did George Washington write this kind of a novel. Oh no. He might have but he did not. He wrote an entirely different kind of a novel.

There are many kinds of a novel even when you know what a novel is.

How can an American marry five women and the last of them be a french woman. The last one was not a french woman but a Swedish woman and she had a great deal of money which she finally lost and married him the American and she thought in marrying him she would begin again having money and they did. He did not have to make money because she soon inherited her own money and then he went away and perhaps he forgot to come back again at any rate she never saw him again.

An American married an indo-chinese woman yes he married her he did not marry a chinese or japanese he married an indo-chinese but told no one and no one told him and there are no other indo-chinese women waiting for him.

What do Americans say when they marry. They say I married her.

Americans marry a woman. Oh yes they do.

If they do they may care to be better than they were.

If an American marries a foreign woman does he remain faithful to her. Very often he does. If he marries an American woman does he remain faithful to her. He very often does.

It is a part of that interesting thing that American men marry American women and have American children. Just yet.

Volume II

To come back to what a novel is. It is rarely that they feel well when it is too late.

But it can be that. A novel can be that. And George Washington, tears, mostly when they wish when they have a wish mostly then they remember that it is not necessary that George Washington should write for them.

It is a strange thing that he felt no tears although everything about him in him for him with him made something that made any one feel something when they told something. Something about him, most assuredly he himself when he himself told anything about him or for him or what he was doing. It was touching as tears are not touching but he dissolved nothing, nothing for nothing. And that made him know what a novel is, what a novel was, as nobody else knew as nobody else can know. Oh yes he knew, he knew what a novel is.

Volume III

AN AMERICAN married an American which was the same as marrying a foreigner and he was very content and had twins.

Volume IV

IF THEY knew what a novel is, how do they know it.

Volume V

Now think what a novel is.

Hamilton is nothing, he was just an Englishman. He was an Englishman in America. He thought he was forming the Federal party but he was not, it was the Americans who were the federal party and he was only a boss, nothing but a boss.

Then there is the Democratic party. There was Cleveland and when America was all through with Cleveland they wanted Cleveland again and there was nothing to it. Then there was Wilson's second term, the democratic party seduces because they only elect a president when they have an exceptional man to elect and a very exceptional man is seductive, no one can help being seduced by an exceptional man.

The Republican party is not seductive because they do not have to have an exceptional man with which to seduce.

George Washington wrote a novel like that and it was a good novel and if any one had the habit they could like reading it. Any habit is a good habit.

Roosevelt Theodore Roosevelt might almost have been a democratic party president, but the reason he was not was that he was not seductive. And his cousin. Well his cousin he was elected because he was just a little seductive, he is seductive, more so, but not enough so, like Smith he sounds more seductive than he is.

But the democratic party is not a failure. It can only be elected when it is seductive and anything that is seductive does not go on again. Not again.

A real failure does not need an excuse. It is an end in itself.

That is what failure is.

Volume VI

AND all this makes me know what I say.

I say that George Washington was the first president of the United States.

I also say that he knew what a novel is.

I also say that he could write a novel every day that is a piece of it every day and everything he had to say with everything he had to say he had to write a piece of a novel every day which he did.

What is a novel.

It is a thing to make you cry if you try.

George Washington never had to try, he never had to cry, but he had to live to die.

And so a novel a novel that he wrote was a very touching novel and he wrote every day and there is no use no use at all in saying that some day the whole novel written every day would be a novel of every day. But it was it certainly was later and just as soon.

He could write and did every kind of a novel.

He could write about war and he could write before a war and he could write a novel of a little war where he was known and a novel about a little war which was what he knew when he wrote his first novels.

How does he like to write novels. He had the novel writing habit. And any habit is a good habit if it is a habit enough that is if it is enough of a habit.

Anybody who has the habit can write a novel and George Washington had the habit of novel writing. It is a habit. Which is soothing, as any habit is which is a habit. And it is touching a habit is touching if any one listens to it as a habit. Oh yes George Washington is very touching and he is the first president of the United States which he was.

No one has made mountains out of meadows and considered meadows as meadows and mountains as mountains. That too is their habit.

In no circumstances can they be better than bitter.

If it is not a habit.

But which they form.

George Washington formed no habit. He had been held and beheld which is not a habit. He wrote his novels which has been a habit. He prepared for his having his wishes which is moreover moreover not a habit and he wrote principally what he had as a future and when it was very well expressed which is also both a habit and not a habit.

But mostly every day he wrote a piece of his novel and that was a habit and it is only thus that a novel can be written.

Which he did.

He was not called any name which begins differently.

He could have had no other name. But then there it is some might be not be.

A child when they have it will grow fatter, very often they worry if it should grow thinner. They had everything to make it thinner and they had it fatter which was a request they made to have it not be thin.

Think of him.

Volume VII

AND then he is not born if it does not matter.

Volume VIII

GEORGE WASHINGTON had no middle name. He will be restless occasionally but very occasionally and never with tears. Nor will he be often cooler. He likes to like just like that.

This may be the history of any younger brother who had been held to be one of a large family.

George Washington loved life and movement and may be often very often without them. They will call it an indifference in wishes. They will pause or they may cloud it altogether. If they may.

They are not anxious.

Please have no pleasure in tears.

It is twice that they are perfect.

George Washington. After all. To be after all. With him. Is a pleasure.

Who has he met. He had met with whom. Should not be silenced.

It is easy to love better. For them or with him. Should it be a fashion. Could he love anything which was a different union. He came again to be often.

This is his history.

What is the difference between history and he likes anything.

I wish to say George Washington can be young. Nobody can ask anything. They cannot ask will you be young.

The first meeting.

The first meeting between George Washington and novel writing.

It had always been there. When he first saw it it was because it had to be as he was young. But very much of course no one can tell which one is young.

Should they be surprised.

No they should not only not be so much as surprised.

This makes many an introduction to many a novel but not such a one as George Washington wrote when he was young.

When he was older and knew what had been true as a novel he did not write that next he wrote another novel. He wrote a novel every day. But not about that because indeed about that no indeed about that.

There could be carelessness enough now.

It was better.

And it could never be now.

George Washington strangely.

I say he knew later that it was not later but now and how.

It is not dangerous.

It is never dangerous as dangerous as distress.

They will come in interest quickly.

And so it happened that it may not end.

Should he be received graciously.

But George Washington was young when he was not received as graciously.

Does anybody remember that he was born in February.

But yes yes of course and so did he and it meant something to him and so he wrote it and as he wrote it it was a novel and he wrote a novel about it.

Or should they complain.

It is not as much.

Do they did they indeed offer it as they went.

All who can remember have seen him.

Volume IX

GEORGE WASHINGTON could change to waiting. But even so every day he did some novel writing.

He had an hour of allowance.

Once unexpectedly.

George Washington was cautious. He met without any hesitation.

And this also kept well in him when every day he wrote a little novel and said what he did say. And what did he say. He said that it was what he did as it was neither held nor withheld from him.

Not and there were never any tears not withheld or withheld from or by him.

And so they can be pressed together.

Held and withheld.

Held and withheld can be pressed together.

This is what can make a novel curious. George Washington did know that.

Finally think that they are beautiful and very little at the first glance.

This is true of any George Washington, which moreover can not connect with his having not said so.

But he wrote so that a novel can move from being young to being young oh yes young.

He was not only not always fair.

His sister was born first as very often happens very delicately.

This could make a novel too. Which is for him for you.

She was made to lie beside her mother so was he and they will be indeed in plenty of meaning which need be in looking up where she is. Very beautifully

How truly a novel speaks.

He is tall. And very small.

George Washington may be entertained by being cautious.

He was ruled by their rest.

Volume X

IT COULD be thought that they could never remember tears.

It could be thought so.

Volume XI

I WISH to mention again that Washington was young.

Naturally not only that but always so. And so. He wrote his novel so. But naturally yes he did.

He wrote it literally. But writing it literally he did not write it so. Not really so.

Everybody can know that he wrote his novel literally and that it was so. And that he was young. Oh yes. So. So young.

Believe me when you hear it.

Volume XII

OR MAY they say.

A very little one may be tiny may be met as the rest. If he is only cautious.

George Washington chose what he would do.

They were careful to think well carefully.

Who could and who did have to.

George Washington never only knew do you do because he lived to like it and have it to do. He was remained.

George Washington comes to live half way through or just as they knew or they did not know.

Who was alike.

If they help they are not very distressing.

It is often their intelligence which is at fault.

George Washington can be called will be or may be they had called him in and it is not a change to bring signs it is by that that they afterward liked it as new.

One of this was that there were not two.

George Washington can not complain. It is better than never.

Volume XIII

THEY never that is he never began a novel with Once upon a time. He always began with having come and he always began it with what happened.

Necessarily they may make you be that for that there is no better remainder which is the same as a reminder of what happened. If you say it every day.

And a novel could not end better than if it could begin.

Oh yes you all know that all who have written a novel and George Washington.

But it is always a nuisance.

He liked it bright. And so did he.

But he naturally did not like it so. He did because he did because he did like it so.

George Washington was not easily not a name.

Not easily.

It is not nearly said. That it is not a name.

But a tittle a title for any of his novels. That is of no importance because after all they come away of themselves. Just as much as more are compared.

Volume XIV

GEORGE WASHINGTON can be when they are not lost in which way to go. He is a boy to be a boy clearly. There is a little that has appeared first but nobody has questioned. In writing and they will ask plainly. Have they been thought to make mention of their being needed more than likely.

And so George Washington is beautifully told.

Who should as they very well say better it with their care.

Once more George Washington is young and ever was.

He writes.

But he does know. What is a novel. Of course he knows what a novel is and tears.

Of course he does.

Volume XV

IT IS not so poignant now.

Now that there are no tears.

Volume XVI

BUT he will add better to better. And so a novel neither dies nor lies.

Volume XVII

BUT which and what did he do.

It made be by and by a sigh.

She sat and it is a warm day.

She sat and read it that way.

Then she took her shoe off.

And put the letter in there.

She did not take care

And she went anywhere.

This is exactly what he did. He had spies and they were faithful to him.

He did write a novel about this.

Which is what he felt as he did.

As he did feel.

Now when they will wish it of all things.

Volume XVIII

HE KNEW I felt about it so that I knew.

George Washington has not only been met but they will think so.

This makes it morally that they are content and contended.

George Washington in relation with a spy will not die.

Which they do.

As their having it could be just once as well.

May they be thou with how they could often leave it as much.

It could be.

Or never change.

In half.

Of the time an allowance.

George Washington never would learn latin and greek lately. But that had nothing to do with how he could use and did use a spy. And if it was to fly he never did nor could nor ever did try to cry.

But he knew how a novel was written. All the same.

And his name.

His name was George Washington.

He would ask partly.

That no one should know that it was indifferent to him what was his name.

That makes a novel. That no one can know that it is indifferent to him to have his name as his name.

This was the way George Washington was.

Otherwise as George he would have had to hear that he knew how a novel could be written anyhow.

I always think of George Washington.

Or prefer. That they could crowd.

It is often that more than which is all is known.

That makes a name allowed.

Three things then now there are to say.

George Washington was born there. Is born there. Lately. As well. But long ago.

Should no one venture to wish.

It could be found finally in extra wishes.

Volume XIX

JUST as well as any one can know that George Washington meaning left to tell them so.

He knew how often they had pride.

They were not there to be left in or without any distress.

In a novel in a good novel there is no distress.

There are spies. One of whom dies. But not while he is a spy. Not to die.

Washington. Sometimes one may forget the name George. But either as George or as Washington he knew very well what a novel is.

And to him to say you know very well what a novel is is no word of reproach.

This is another way to wait.

George Washington oh see.

He was charmed with the dresses of the little baby.

George Washington a little. Can be added to him. As he leaves. Allowing for the window. Or with. Cannot be. As extra.

It is quite how or which George Washington can be who.

If he had a brother so slowly. He did not know.

George Washington for instance does not like George and certainly not when pronounced by a frenchman.

This could or did not make a novel. It is a little matter and could not so quickly or as quickly make a novel.

One must know what can make a novel. And he did.

If he did not who did. But he did. He was nearly as ready as when and if he did.

This makes it be very interesting that he knew how many are called by each name. So many are called George even George Washington is called George.

But not as easily as a novel.

It is more easy for George Washington to write a novel than to be called George but he was called George as often just the same.

They feel practically as well about this as they do about anything.

But very often they do not know what to do. But if you have a novel to write you always do know what to do.

Oh yes you do.

He did.

And his name was George and although about this there was perfect agreement it was not at all or really interesting.

This was the way he managed to begin.

To begin makes no one restless. But he was not restless and he went on. He was not told how often he tried but he never tried. The french army may never be tired but he George Washington never tried.

In which case there is no use in being careful as well as famous. And he was both.

He knew what a novel is and he could and he did write one and some.

But at nobody's request.

He knew what a novel is.

What has George got to do with it.

Everything and nothing.

And from and nearly we begin.

Begin then.

Volume XX

GOOD-BYE George was never said to George Washington.

Oh may why. Be returned.

The simple story. Is. That as a child who was born, which, it, came first.

And neither how or. Perhaps never.

That makes it agreeable that, Good-bye George was not said to George Washington.

I would like George Washington.

The birth of George Washington.

He is not born.

A very pretty charming boy came to be born in the place of which no one could fancy that it had come.

Alright.

Could all be here who heard that he was here not here.

Volume XXI

ANY evening that he went away some one could say good-bye George and could say Good-bye George was not what was said to George Washington.

And so George Washington cried.

Not only. Within itself. Because alternately. He was not coming. Nor had he come. Nearly enough.

Has no one been to see George Washington.

And if they did. Would they as they did say good-bye George as he was leaving.

All this makes any one think just how Mount Vernon looked when he threw a stone across. And nobody said and it makes one careless nobody said to George Washington good-bye George when they left even as they did not say good-bye George when he left.

Do you see how all this makes him write the novels he did. They were good novels too and they were very true.

They were just as true as just to say that if and he certainly did go away nobody said good-bye George as he went away.

And so a novel was prepared.

And he wrote it.

No one has been to see him when he went away.

Should they be certain to be known to be just as well-known. As they will reason. Could it be better. Just a little baby first. He came. They said they knew his name. They said it was George Washington. They did not say then to him none of them said it to him then, good-bye George.

But afterward they were not satisfied.

Should any one leave guessing or reason to them.

George Washington was one of wishes. It is.

That makes it be habitable apart. I mean Mount Vernon and a novel.

A novel is written as a story that is in a scene one of two.

By this which they are rich.

Volume XXII

It is very ordinary which is the same as quite extraordinary that a novel needs no place to part. They cannot part. That is how it happens that nobody can say good-bye George to George Washington.

That makes them remember it there.

He knows what a novel is.

Of course he does.

Which he does because if he does he does know what a novel is.

And what is a novel.

A novel is every day or part of a day and when it happens and if it does which they will place where it is. This is what he did and so he wrote and the novel was written.

Do please please him by saying the novel was written.

But he knew.

Because he wrote all day and if he wrote all day which he did the novel was written

Prepare any way you like.

Once more how did he go about it.

No one or no.

That is not what he said.

He wrote a novel and so he had no no. He accepted what he said and so did he and Mount Vernon.

With love for them to have it know.

Just what was happily all or more so.

No one need ask him what a novel is.

This is what he knew. What a novel is.

Oh do you like whatever you say.

A novel may happen to have half the time but really a novel and George Washington knew that it was so had to has to have all the time.

And so nobody and how well everybody knows it said good-bye George when he went away.

George is promised.

Be wise for George. Ought you to be ought too. It is well named.

Once in a while they like to go and to have it told so. He might be pleasea o again. And so. They lay.

George Washington had plenty of time and this is not only not un-favorable but it is necessary otherwise how can you know that is who knew what a novel is if it is so.

A novel is not so and so oh no.

A novel is favorably that they need not only to do so but that they do do so.

And George Washington was well arranged as to a place and places all the places.

So a novel as novel went on not only to begin but to have begun. It even ended so.

That is what they like. It even ended so. Tears do not flow. That is it is as it is ended so.

He may be gathered faster.

That is they may be slow to know.

But it is true. That once in every way each novel ended so. He wrote not a great number but a number of them.

Volume XXIII

WHICH leads not singularly to ways of narrative.

Volume XXIV

FORT NECESSITY does not separate a novel from reality.

Really really.

And if an Indian is a scout who may they be.

They may be not friends but not alone friends.

And so. Nobody who wrote a novel was not alone.

Once more in feeling felt in tears not fears.

And if he came and if he went away.

And no one ever did say. As he went away. Good-bye George.

Volume XXV

WHICH leads not as singularly to ways of narrative.

Is narrative a novel. Yes when it is accompanied by these facts. The facts that they did what they did which they did when they were accompanied.

I remember so well how they lived as well not having been dead.

Nobody could prepare truth from death. And nobody could kill. Him.

He was George Washington and he had to wait. But it was not to wait. Because he did and this is what is what he did. He wrote. And the novel or novels he wrote. There are two things spoke and wrote. He wrote. That makes novels. Oh yes he wrote.

Volume XXVI

CAPTAIN JACK or the wild hunter of the Juniata said that George Washington would write.

He did right.

Volume XXVII

HE WROTE because this did lead not only regularly but very nearly to all ways of narration.

And that makes novel reading. Why does it not.

If he does as he did if not why not.

But he certainly did. George Washington as certainly did.

Volume XXVIII

GEORGE WASHINGTON was as religious in no appearances.

Need or knew a church. In which not one who went saw. Which it had been just as well as known.

Refusing or accepting being or leaving George Washington knew that any way through he had to have it there in his novel. A novel of any day in his life is a novel. Which is it. It is his novel which he wrote. Nobody cares how he writes his novel but write his novel he must and he does. Was and does and never tears.

But it can be so moving. As if not only he knew but it was too. Just as much as ever.

No one should not remember that he was born first.

At first.

George Washington can be called one. And they will come to-morrow. Oh how horrid it is to be not allowed to have been both the younger and the elder. Which is it. Do you not like it. Will you not mind it. Will you not get it. Do you not have it. George Washington naturally could be in uniform. He was waiting.

That is the way I he knew what a novel is.

All who are prepared like not to say that they will add a wedding to-day. After it a little of it was born. Should they like it. If they are through. Or yes.

This is the way what he wrote. What is it he wrote. What is the difference between written and wrote. That is what is the difference between cries and tries.

Oh use a novel as a day.

George Washington should be often quietly. Not by it.

Volume XXIX

IF SOME ONE stands where it stood and there is no light where it was and within there it is within there and he is seen. It is not why they say never to be forgotten.

A novel can not be made more than all at once. As he knew.

And so there are a great many there. There where he made novels share share being there.

Any novel likes being all there.

He wrote them.

George Washington was seen to ask his mother.

She could not say no nor as yet yes. It was too soon.

George Washington would prefer yesterday or to-morrow he knows which is better and which is a choice. They will be once in a while guilty of no distress.

They like to have it done. They like it one and one. One and one never makes two. If there there too. Just now there is one. When will there be another one.

George Washington as one.

And call it Washington. Or one of not two.

They will never know it by name.

Volume XXX

WHO can be fortunate.

Could it be sweet to congratulate.

Sweetly will they be placed.

Do think why they wait.

They have not known for which.

He had one. He was not known.

He had her child or two.

He could just smile if he was born already. Or he. Should just smile. If he was born already. Is it not strange that it was Washington's birthday to-day. And he was not born. Oh indeed no he was not born.

Volume XXXI

JUST as we see that he had been left already as he was young. There is this a difference between young and begun and well and strong.

I think you see that George Washington had it to say to be that he had been born. As he was born he had been young not young to be born but young. And yet as a novel in a novel are they as young are they as born we may say as he was.

Completely nearly as he was.

Will George Washington be three of two.

No.

One two three with him. It is easy to make a mistake. And to be mistaken.

What was he mistaken for. He was not mistaken. How was he not mistaken.

He could not be mistaken because he is and was and so is a novel and so is he. Not one of two or three.

He was the one with a novel to write and he wrote every day and to be every day as a novel a day it is necessary very necessary to be an age of an age. It is also very necessary to always have something young. It is always very necessary to have something not all if ever older than not young. Oh yes all this is necessary enough. And any one can know that George Washington is so.

George Washington was mistaken. They placed him where. If he had been. He would not have been indifferent. Nor would they have been different. But they liked a loss.

But every moment was not the same.

I could easily remember the name of George but I do not. Not any generation can not. Can not not remember the name of George.

There is no difference between how do you do and how do you know.

Do you see why George a while.

George Washington was especial to George.

George Washington had not to be had by a mother.

George who. Will have no care for you. It is better to have come again. He will come.

Will it will he with they be just with it with him with one as restless.

Can a novelist be restless. Is writing a novel restless. No not at all and so George Washington he wrote. He wrote as many novels. Not as many as days not as many as years but he wrote as many.

Why will they shine with all their might.

Could he not having yet been known around like it that at no age could they say have to add it. Can it be likely that they will be older if they see it. See carries across or by having been afterwards made to come as welcome. Change one to one. And they do not know.

It is easy to know George Washington because in that way he can be written. He writes for that to tell it to be so. Any novel does oh yes any novel does.

Will they be true or through before or who.

This makes a memory of it all.

Food for which they had not bought it and this be George Washington's care. Once in a while they come again just as they like. Why is George Washington cautious.

Anything makes no difference all the same.

But having it to do did he do it.

Of course he did.

And of course if he was dead he was not dead. Not as dead.

George Washington was not meant for two.

Now think what a novel is.

All you who know think do try do think what a novel is.

George Washington knew. He knew it too. He did know what a novel is and he was used to it. He was very well planned to be used to it.

Volume XXXII

BUT why by why but why will he go.

Or but why did he not come.

Or but why did he come and come.

Volume XXXIII

GEORGE WASHINGTON was not jealous. He knew what a novel is. He knew that there are characters in a novel.

Georges are often known.

This is a question for a guess.

Was he or was he a guess. And will he guess. Of course he will. How likely.

He shall be left to be only here. He shall be not only left.

This is a question for a guess. And to guess yes.

If he knew that there are characters in a novel and of course he knew that he could not be jealous.

Not nearly why they abide by what they like yet.

Or. Which they mean to pause.

George Washington is known as not to minister to their being without them.

All this works together to make it be known that he knew what a novel is.

He may be one although he has not as yet come.

In this light he was as young as young as a novelist is.

He may well be well born. And he. He is.

He was very warm when they were very cold.

Or the other way round.

But this is not the way in which they show that they are either young as young as he can be or not.

A novelist can and has been young. Not young enough but young.

Should a novelist be thought to be anxious not to be born first.

George Washington need have had no anxiety over that.

Listen to what George Washington can say.

Which leads not singularly to the ways.

I looked and looked and saw. And it was a pleasure if I looked and it was at what I looked and saw.

There is no hesitation in knowing George Washington was young.

This may make it soon may be they could be well soon.

If he is as young.

Volume XXXIV

IT MOVES as lack of like a moon and they will praise it as as soon. And this was why they changed their hope of making it be ready yet for you.

It was so easy just to like it.

Volume XXXV

I WISH to commence again to have their pause.

If he was young and he was how young was he.

That is as you feel about it.

When they exacted little descriptions what did they see.

They saw that nobody said it was ready to be ready to be left.

In any sense a novel is a novel. In any sense of the word.

Think not only of his life but why he had a name. Think not only of why he had a name but why name does rhyme with fame. Think not only of why his name does rhyme with fame. Think only of how to think of nothing else.

There all who announce announce what they know. But do they know. If they know what a novel is do they know.

He does and can know because it is not a pause not as a pause.

He knows what a novel is not only because every day because of every day but because of periods of parts of every day.

Now I have this to say yesterday as well as yesterday for yesterday and to-day.

I say that they like what I say.

Now here listen what a novel is.

I say that it is true that looking just like you makes it be better that it is not only true that when they say they may that here and there it is best to be sure that they will be best of any often may they be apprised of how often they can be called. Will you come and be careful.

Volume XXXVI

I THINK this is why I like to come and look and make it be just as much theirs as most. An easy delay does not make it ask of it to be what they fancy as diminishes.

I could like a simple walk in life and no deceptions.
But they will please talk alike.
And he may rest when he labors.
It is I hope that I understand and hope to know all of which he says.
I wish to say that the way they tell that they are well is this.

Volume XXXVII

A NOVEL is do not fancy that everybody knows do not fancy that they have to go do not fancy that they build what is there do not fancy that parts of it are different, do not fancy that they do not look alike, do not fancy that they please us, do not fancy that they should object, do not fancy that they call when or as they come do not fancy that this place is not a place for that do not fancy that they should spoil that do not fancy that they have this do not fancy what they like.

A novel may be not be theirs any more.

But this was not at all what happened to George, George could not carry but he could which there is to have done carry all.

By this means there is no use if fortunately they willed that he could do that and just as much more.

They felt no hope.

This all of this makes a novel have a place.

But this was not what he did. Not George as Washington.

Could any George be George as Washington.

That makes neither a novel nor a fact.

George was not George as Washington.

He was George Washington nevertheless.

Nevertheless is not useless.

Let me have George Washington please.

George Washington sometimes it is surprising, George Washington knows what a novel is.

He had this which he had to do.

And if you wish very well.

Do you if you wish very well think very well.

Some of which do.

I think it is all very clear and now how about it.

George Washington does does do what a novel is.
Every day one day.
This may be why they like it.
Now Abraham Lincoln did not do what a novel is.
I hope you can see that George Washington does.

Volume XXXVIII

WILL two think two will.

Volume XXXIX

THEY could be heard asking why they fastened. Nobody says what. In which they play. Oh do be gracious as well as cautious.

I have been thinking of why they know there is a difference between what they like and what they like to hear.

Also how often. They will say how often they will say they will fasten it, as they will like which is more than they come.

Nobody hesitates with George Washington.

There is no sense in asking.

Or might he think it was for him.
Who does not ask whom.
There is no difference between dim and him.
Oh join or join in just as much as may.
They allow for which.

But George Washington does not need any allowance. Nobody who knows what a novel is does.

They may be content to wonder yet will they not have to have it made to-day as well as yesterday.

This can be their belief in no rectification.

Nobody who knows what a novel is needs that.

I think well of not only telling a thing twice may be.

Volume XL

IT COULD interest him in them to him that it came.
But no.

Why not.
Let us leave ours as best and better.
There is no why not.
It is not an inconvenience.
I think that I was pleased that I understood what I saw.
No head no thread.
This is a case of their leaving.

Volume XLI

Now a little time in which to rest.

Volume XLII

I HAVE seen that by looking I knew what I knew.
That is just yes.
That may be their way in their way.
It can happen.
Can happen that he standing there is remaining.
Not when they like
It is by no means renewable that as you walk the street and see a policeman even if you do not notice any one that you wish that you might know that all the same it is all the same.
This is a novel too.
This is what George Washington knew.
He did not know it there but he knew.
And if in any way there is no way.
There is no way in which there is any way.
His way.
It is all too precautious.
But no change where.
I could I would I should.
They may as well care.
Fall means fall or fallen.
But any novel is true.
And they like out loud with clouds.

And so very well may you.

Which he may very really save for them alone.

Which he may very really save for kind

Any novel can make any one cry.

How can an hour be their own alone.

It may be best that he has had to write.

A novel.

By his day.

And but it is.

He could be always ready.

He might or might not say, I could be always ready.

He will do much alone.

He may be thought to be rich this is how often this is.

Volume XLIII

PLEASE prepare to be prepared to be ready to be.

And he was.

See here does or does not that make a novel.

Of course which it does.

It is of no anxiety to be restless when they awoke.

It is of no anxiety no pressing anxiety not to be or to be restless when he awoke.

He knew George Washington knew.

Think how you can lose a name.

George Washington might be some one and that one was one who was not the one.

So George Washington can lose one lose one as a name.

And then there.

A novel is there.

Because if any one has written the novel of that one no one no not any one can lose any such a one.

Well why do you come in often when they are strong.

This makes it less like this.

I wish you or any one would think this about any one and George was such a one George Washington was not or ever any one because he knew he really truly knew he all but knew he well completely well knew he knew it all through just what a novel is.

I have often thought that I have often come to walk can be written of any one.

George Washington never said he was through.

He never said all should be shared as yellow and blue.

They may just as well as wishes.

Does it make no difference what they do.

All this leads not to fellow but to very well I tell you.

What could Washington say if he were not well known.

He could say.

Every year they make more than they made but this not only does make anybody well to wish.

Begin again.

All this does not make any one very well known.

Very well known. George Washington is very well known.

Volume XLIV

AND now I ask you how many feel well for me.

Volume XLV

THIS makes an add and an embellishment which he likes very much. This is why he reads print.

He writes very well and he tells about how he wishes.

This is their increase.

Volume XLVI

COMMENCE now.

Volume XLVII

A PLAN to have a novel follow.

Volume XLVIII

How they did not ask him what he thought.

What is a romance.

Oh be with me without an adventure. And they will very likely go and see it.

I think so.

George Washington did not know what an adventure is but he did go and see it and as he saw it he was in the midst of it.

As he was in the midst of it it was as if he had been to see it.

As he had been not to see it but engage in it it was not only necessary that it was not a romance but a novel.

Do you see for which do you see.

At the entrance of the bay a bay is a body of water not surrounded entirely by land he knew that they were to go straight through.

He knew about this too if it were a lake.

Do you see the difference between a novel and romance.

Oh how often do they wish and wish and wishes.

But he was never through.

To be through is to be done with.

But in a novel there is never done with because there is always a sequel.

That is true.

George Washington was true.

He was never through.

Oh yes there is a difference between a romance and adventure and a novel.

But which is best.

George Washington is best.

East and west.

George Washington is best.

No one need leave out north and south. Not for him.

Pleasing is not pressed.

There is no because in pleasing.

What he wishes to say is this.

That he had to do what a novel is never through.

And a novel is never begun.

What, do they not tell all they know. They do not tell all they know because they know that any others others may or may not go and they may or may not or might not say go. Or might not say so.

What is the reason that a commencement is in vain.

This is why when he looked at one and one of each one or another he was not only unprepared.

That is the reason that a commencement is in vain.

Volume XLIX

SOLEMNLY.

This leads me gradually.

Volume L

AFTER a while he knew what pauses were.

Volume LI

As THEY walk more than just to and fro, as they were plan to have a better Dan. They may never know.

They may never walk more than just to and fro.

But George Washington had no walking to do.

This which is this a novel which is this not walking to and fro not planning for a Dan, but they may never plan or plan just so.

A novel does not arrange anything.

A novel is that they need never know.

Do they repair despair.

This then a novel need not ever know.

Sometimes when a bay is known they have no plan.

George Washington knew that a discovery makes a plane they know and a novel can be any share of neither where or there.

That is what a novel is. It is which they came.

He never overcame.

That is what a novel is.

Volume LII

HE KNEW what a novel is what money is.

And so he was perfectly powerless with well well be or not be astonished.

He said he never said come quickly.

He said come quickly.

All of which made nobody made a mistake and so it looks like it

What is it when they say they will rest while they look like it.

This is their change.

And so he could and did know that as so many things happened they will not buy more than if it were just that.

This is a full explanation of why they looked together. All of which is information or a narrative.

But not a novel.

This is why they question early if they have come early.

Because it is not a novel.

George Washington he knew what a novel is.

Volume LIII

WHAT is the system they say that ought ought to be may they.

This is a narrative as an index.

What to do about a narrative.

When George Washington told what he had done it might have been a narrative but it was not. It was not a narrative because it had not been begun.

It was a novel because it had not been begun.

It is of no interest to know about it.

Could it be well to be always here to be always here to be always here could it be well to be always here just as they were at that time.

And so it is so when they are behind with their work.

This is what makes George Washington a novel and not a narrative because not having begun he was not behind in his work.

What is what they do not write. They do not write that they knew.

And just so is more than which they had when it is not often.

George.

What a name is George.

What an average is George.

What a land is George.

What a novel is George.

George is not a narrative.

And what could not he have been.

Because no George could have been begun it is not in the nature of a George.

Nor could he be behind in his work not a George and so he could not be a narrative not a George.

Could he say every day it looked alike which he was welcome.

It is better to be so tender.

Volume LIV

WHAT had not George Washington said.

That is why they like his and made.

It is often thought that love and war may be careful. Just now we have known two doors. One door is for a door.

There is only one door because George Washington never wore a door. No he did not wear, wear what they like.

It was a pleasure to think that he did this for him.

What is the best thing they can do the best thing they can do is to buy something.

This makes narrative that is what they are telling not at a stand-still.

All which they mean

Tell any one.

Volume LV

Now I have nothing more to say about how George Washington can tell to-day that he wrote six novels before he was thirty-five.

Six of them and that is not a great many.

How very soon does one not care that they were there from there or to here or from here to there which perhaps just like it they do or do not change.

This is what I think.

Which he says.

George Washington does not say he he says.

This is what he says.

It does not matter who has come when they have only been called first.

He is very grateful that they listen not by themselves.

He says all this.

The story which he told he told they do not care who to care.

This is what he says.

Let me say just why I came.

Again this is what he says.

I come because she is waiting.

And she comes also.

This is what he says George Washington says.

Leave me to say whatever I like.

George Washington says.

I have felt when I have seen them that they were often there.

George Washington did not say.

It is not by the time that there is a cloud of out loud.

No he did not say so.

But he might of.

Of course he might of.

Of course he might have even if although he did not say so.

I should be very pleased to have them be anxious about me.

He might have come to say so.

It was in this way that it was not now.

That too he might have come to say oh yes to say.

Now this is all the difference between what is and what was.

Which he did which he did come to say which as he did come to say so.

One need not do it but it should be done.

Which as he did he did say so.

Did one who had the name of George come to say so.

George Washington came to say so.

The George Washington come to say so.

In this way slowly it turns not away and not ever from not being yesterday.

So George Washington can come to has come to say so.

He has been thinking that what makes them this is this.

This is what a novel is.

Volume LVI

WHAT was Washington that made it right for him to be all that.

Is there anybody who does not know that the city of Washington was named after him.

Is there.

Oh yes there is

At one time if they were sitting and not under a leafy tree not at all, it was as their custom.

All of which is right

As Washington George Washington always is

Volume LVII

IT IS very singular to be often after they went away.

This is what Washington George Washington can say.

Volume LVIII

AND now think how it came that he was interested.

Volume LIX

ANOTHER thing he said.

It is best to know that it is so very often that they will not count. I know how they feel just after every hundred.

Volume LX

THERE should be just these reflections in a novel.

It is very likely that love will follow which they call me.

Now listen carefully to how they felt now which they knew.

It makes no difference whether he will order or be loved.

It is well known which is why he said.

He will be practiced very likely in why they came.

I like a way to cherish.

Which he said.

Volume LXI

GEORGE WASHINGTON is not head long or steadfast.

He is not held by it at last.

He is not meant to be and not to fast.

But they might like it best.

Best and most is most and best.

This is what George Washington meant when he sent them away.

Oh all who know George Washington believed him.

Volume LXII

AFTER waiting and they know will they will they tell it so. To their great astonishment he did.

Washington did.

George Washington did.

It was told correctly.

I wish to ask is it of any interest now.

George Washington had rather had said that he knew rather that he had said.

And so George Washington had said.

This is where after thirty five he did write more novels.

The next one began like this.

A man who can be known often known each as will again I have lost all which they have fastened mildly now why do they add in obstruction it is not which for which they can outlast.

Then George Washington wrote another one and this one when it was begun was this.

How will they hand or handle what they have not been thought to know.

Then he George Washington wrote another one and this other one when it began was begun like this one.

I wish to leave intelligently for it now.

Then he George Washington was not done he did begin another one.

It is often what they like that makes them leave it alone.

It is when he hears that he knows flattery. He said he liked it.

All who are gained are cursed with their own being a pleasure.

Volume LXIII

I WISH to say that all true stories when they follow an advertisement are exciting.

As also when they explain why a man is named half after a flower in dislike.

More also because it is too told that they will heighten by not all alone.

He could be only known to cloud.

George Washington could wish to say that he could understand him.

George Washington could not say.

Well wish it for me wish it for me that I had rather not had hand made.

This George Washington can say.

No one who has been seen has been cautious.

Volume LXIV

GEORGE WASHINGTON can say.

Let me always know that a cow can chew his cud or her cud.

Because George Washington specialises like that.

Volume LXV

IF IT is possible to know that a monkey came down from a man not a man from a monkey and this is so as perhaps it is so that when they find a man in America surrounded by elephants and reptiles and others there is no monkey.

And this is the background of America from George Washington to Bryan.

And they are right.

How they are capable to have it change.

If they that is if he could leave it alone all the time they would be as white while they were there.

Let us think how happy we are.

Just then they were related.

George Washington was related.

The basis of knowing what a novel is is that the monkey is a degenerated man from a man not man from a monkey.

And that was what related is.

And that is what a novel is.

And George Washington knew what a novel is.

And he lived his life as a man as an American man and thus he knew what a novel is and he wrote a great many, truthfully and not begun.

Oh yes not begun.

This makes it do that they will not partly tell differently from which one is who is who.

Who is who is not what they have to do.

George Washington.

Who is who.

And what can he do.

He can write the work as well as he did do.

He did do what he did do.

Who is who is what he did do.

And this makes living less not a failure.

Nor does it make living less a success.

Nor does it make living less nevertheless.

George Washington was never living less, no one who knows what a novel is does.

He could be thought to say it all the same. But not that.

Who could say can you see.

He did not say if you can do you see.

He said.

After I read I was not certain that they lived Easter for me.

He also said.

I wish to say that no one was more anxious.

Volume LXVI

It is in every way a happiness not to seize it first.

Volume LXVII

GEORGE HAWKINS is a name that goes with George.

George Washington is a name.

And so they need never know who told them so.

Or which on their account.

All fortunately are told out loud.

Or they may be often occasioned to need no one apiece.

And so who is who is all to you.

George Washington was thought.

He could say.

I like everything that happens for them for Monday.

He could not say

And so they know why they know out loud.

He could think.

It is very extraordinary that they are not more here than there which they do.

This he could be to have no one better. That is George Washington.

In this to say slowly that he knew where they went.

George Washington had a way but no one can say nor he. And this is the way.

It is well to be here and not only not here but where.

They were painstaking in and on their account.

George Washington could say and that led in a way.

I would like to know just why they were principally there.

At least it came to be very well George Washington came to be very well to wish or not to wish and this he did say which it was to wish.

Just now I feel that they will not only tell but not be made to be helpful just why they wish.

Volume LXVIII

THIS was when many thought the same.

Volume LXIX

BUT if they did not was there anybody at all who was to blame.

Volume LXX

GEORGE WASHINGTON thought not.

Volume LXXI

HE was angry without a wish.
 This is why everything is changed and they are not to wish again.

Volume LXXII

WHAT can all who have been George Washington be.
 What can all who have been George Washington do.
 There is no answer to that.

Volume LXXIII

THE reason that May makes them anxious is that they have been as anxious.
 But April will do.
 And who who prefers February.
 In this way March misses.
 But George Washington did march.
 Oh yes and as anxious and as anxiously no oh yes.
 Any other thing which they have been as anxious about is just this.

Volume LXXIV

GEORGE WASHINGTON.

Volume LXXV

FOR a fought.
 But which they ought.

Volume LXXVI

GEORGE WASHINGTON

Volume LXXVII

OR WHY not be careful

Volume LXXVIII

GEORGE WASHINGTON.

Volume LXXIX

HE HAS heard it rumored that it was not true.

It could be often said that it is often not there that they are better than even without this.

And so they will kiss.

There is no kiss without careful feeling for peace.

And so George Washington knew all he knew.

And all he knew was true.

That is what a novel is.

Volume LXXX

ALL who are often thought of could and could and better here than there.

Volume LXXXI

GEORGE WASHINGTON.

Volume LXXXII

IT IS all mine, coming too fluently.

PART TWO

Volume LXXXIII

GEORGE WASHINGTON.

Volume LXXXIV

HE HAS a great hesitation in often too.

In very likely.

What is the difference between hearing and seeing if both may acclaim, oh oh Bartholemew.

Bartholemew has nothing to do with George Washington because Bartholemew did not know what a novel is and George Washington is he is to know what a novel is.

What has he had to say.

It is often there that they are very happy.

In which way they changed as much.

He thinks with Bartholemew that he will regret it all through.

But he does not.

And why does he not.

Because he knows what a novel is.

Volume LXXXV

HE HAS often thought that if they think of him they think of him as George Washington.

George Washington was young and as young.

He was not begun.

He was as he is.

It is always less as a use.

Or however clouded.

Volume LXXXVI

WHO will be called better nearer.

Volume LXXXVII

OR WHO may they be outwardly.

No wish to wish all of which for Bartholemew.

But George Washington was fairer.

All dogs are like dogs. So George Washington says.

Then if then then if they do not know when, so George Washington says.

Once very often he knew that it was at their plane in their plane but not noticed as for him.

He is meant.

All of which they know as best.

Or which they might as well finish

Which he did.

He knows that a novel finishes and he finishes. There are many novels not begun but he finishes.

George Washington may often be just the same.

What has George Washington thought.

George Washington is not the cause of everything nor will they manage it just now.

But if he is.

But if he is

Volume LXXXVIII

ONE or two of which there is no cause to speak easily.

Volume LXXXIX

GEORGE WASHINGTON has not spoken, nor has Bartholemew.

It is often not only by their choice but by necessity.

Volume XC

GEORGE WASHINGTON was well and well again.

Volume XCI

No DO not think well of them.

Volume XCII

GEORGE WASHINGTON was when they had to say that he did not have it in any way to say not to-day.

This is what he said.

No do not think well of them

Once upon a time they were not afraid to have it known that it came again.

During which time they may have thought or not thought of ought.

It was their meaning they withdrew from them. In the meantime. And very soon across to throw.

Think how George Washington can link. Link this with that.

How should anything thrown be framed.

Volume XCIII

A PLAN which they have may not bother George Washington.

He asked them to be his. Or rather may they happen to order milk.

If they were ready may he deduce from this preparation.

Or rather may they tell it as very likely.

It is very robust to be well aware of why they were ready.

Just now.

George Washington was born but they not only let no one know but they waited.

Volume XCIV

WITH which it went it was as well-known that they went often

George Washington did not come nor was it just as well that he went. He was sent.

George Washington may not be changed because they come.

They will not only hope not to differ to expect him. But of this it is quite certain.

Oh why will they like not only known so much.

This is a cry from the heart or from where the heart is not only of George Washington but of any novelist and George Washington was a novelist and knew what a novel is.

Think kindly of use of so much.

Or more narrowly in tears.

But in a novel there is no mention of tears not if they knew what a novel is and George Washington did he did know what a novel is and he wrote a great many of them just as many as he did as he did write.

If they will like it again.

That is another thing he said and thought George Washington said and George Washington thought.

It is of no importance that they are only not only not selfish.

This is not only what George Washington said and George Washington thought.

In no man's memory.

Volume XCV

YES who can doubt the truth of their attempt.

Volume XCVI

OR WHICH one fails.

Volume XCVII

THEY may like it.

Volume XCVIII

ABOUT when will they come.
    After as he intended to like.
    Better than it.
    For them it is no fortune.
    On their account.
    This is what George Washington is.

Volume XCIX

I THINK I will sell a wheel a day in this way they who are awkward are not supplied.

Volume C

ALL this is in the beginning not all the truth.
    But George Washington was not begun.
    And so and so to speak it is the truth.

Volume CI

FULL of why they ask.

Volume CII

ONCE more and once more when, George Washington.

Volume CIII

EACH one is perfect when two are enough.

Volume CIV

ONCE more when they went again to or for Washington.

Volume CV

ONE can almost forget that Washington is George Washington but not enough. He was George Washington.

Volume CVI

Now he need not tell you what he is trying to do.

Once when they were willing they were just as complete as ever.

Once when they were willing they were just as comfortable as ever.

Not more than George Washington.

Not more comfortable than George Washington.

Volume CVII

HE WAS anxious to know it. George Washington was. He was anxious to know it.

It is often that they please.

He was anxious to know it.

When they may be cautious they may not be anxious.

He was not anxious about that George Washington was not anxious.

Once when they were all older George Washington was not cared for.

He was not anxious about that.

It is not known just why he was anxious.

It is not only their hope but also their anxiety that filled them they were pleased to be always there and not to be lost just yet.

George Washington was not anxious also.

For instance if they were anxious they were equally not wanting to have it be known then.

George Washington had no anxiety to be anxious.

May be all those who were welcome were not only thought of but with it they had not nearly enough or some of it which is what they had as an example.

As such George Washington was remarkable.

In which case not only was it of no use.

All this makes it fairly clear why George Washington was not begun as he was not.

Neither is a novel begun.

All this makes this fairly clear

And indeed moreover it does make it fairly clear that George Washington was a novelist and knew what a novel is. Is or was.

George Washington is a place for which there can be no mistake.

He is helped with them as they found which it is in their plane.

Which it is in their case.

George Washington can write that and he can write that in his hand-writing.

They knew that they were to have been here in not their way only but also why they left.

This too he can write George Washington can write.

It is hopeful to let George Washington know.

Should he not be well-known not to wait.

It is very soon that they know a noon at noon.

This too in his hand-writing is as written.

All which he knew when he went away.

But he as he was never went away because as he was he never went away.

This he did not say.

George Washington did not say this because this is this and a novelist has not this to say. And George Washington was a novelist and he wrote a novel day by day. That is what a novel is.

George Washington was one of the cases which he had in mind. Or not to get away from which they meant.

It is often the father of which he is the father who is persistent.

Or more than how they like.

It is often that they thought well of it.

This is all as they had it to say about George Washington about Washington as they say. To say.

George Washington did not say and if he did did he say.

They will strangely play as they know it very well.

Did he say this.

If he did it had nothing to do with his novel writing.

He may be not at all like it.

But he was.

If at no time, but he was.

And one of any one.

What of it all is true

No one can say but Washington did.

Did you see how I wrote out here.

George Washington was not only known down there.

He was not born. Oh how do you do. He was not born.

Volume CVIII

HE AROUND a view by which by this time all for they may not have chosen it is all bought.

All of which to all of which they agree.

All of which they agree.

They may think that Louis Henry James and Marius will replace George but not at all it will not and yet it is very difficult to make a sacrifice.

George Washington need not have joined or made it all a pleasure.

Who can be so glad that George is not there where Louis is.

It is their own for which they are remarkable.

He would never he would never lose his place.

Volume CIX

GEORGE WASHINGTON had a habit any novelist has of needing what he had.

He said there is an age between and they will need they will need to know the age between. This age between makes it recognisable.

Flowers make George Washington careless he never won to name.

He never need never win to name what a flower is if he does he does know what it is.

This makes no difference if there is an age between.

He made this be because there always was a novel which he wrote.

He knew that it was not only here that they were born.

He knew he knew that it was always their plain as plain for them, not frugal but an instance.

That is what a novel means an age is not an age it is between an age. Oh yes it is.

George Washington knew what to do.

Volume CX

To THINK two not two.

What would the poor orphans do if there was no military service.

This has nothing to do with George Washington or the disturbance of a rolled ball.

This was the way he was surrounded.

It is easy for it to be the way he was surrounded.

This too has to do with what he did do.

What did he do.

It is very warm if it is not very hot for Bartholemew.

Yes dress well.

George Washington.

Nobody needs close doors for him because he will naturally win.

Oh yes he won.

George Washington will not say that when it did come to pass they would not only happen to stay which they did. He knows how to comfort.

That is what a novel is.

It is a comfort.

George Washington entitled would he or would he not eat pigeon or which he chose when he was deprived.

Nobody likes what he likes.

George Washington may meant to mean him.

From which they thank him from this that indeed better than capability Washington understood too that they should not be patient because of whatever they could or could not do.

No one changes George Washington to hope.

Volume CXI

Or would they do well to relish it.

Volume CXII

He sleeps accompanied by a dog while it rains on a Sunday afternoon this makes that they neglect George Washington for whom a bird sings birds sing or not sing because they like the time George Washington has been heard.

George Washington may be fought for just why they should wish for this.

George Washington do they separate them from not with them or kindly let well enough alone.

It is often that they think not why they were known.

Volume CXIII

This is not why a novel thinks.

Not why not.

If George Washington met a woman and she was well to do would she be a woman who had been busy as a woman is busy who is and has done more than that in being there when it is not only best but necessary to do it so that there is nobody else there or not.

This is that way and that way is the way a novel thinks.

George Washington is exact.

In wishes they may be rich in wishes and riches for them for which they have gone.

This is the way George Washington thinks. This is the way a novel thinks.

George Washington may marry a ball.

George Washington may not be ferocity as well yesterday.

Or they will as who like George Washington will or will or who like George Washington they make it please extras better than more of which it is alike because of the George Washington they met because he will be well at least for then they can in because not begun more not one or George Washington which may name two play two again they think what it is not only why not they mean fourteen mean.

What can it mean not in between. Between ages. Yes ages is what there is to mean.

George Washington can mean.

Volume CXIV

IT IS not only known I think I should mention George Washington soon may be they do say it is as soon in July too George Washington in no case when it is not theirs to try.

George Washington not, neither or, added was he glad.

That is what makes a novel especially.

Why is it all they like in George Washington.

Order it for George Washington which is not only right but may be not only but at least perhaps will be what they cannot keep from learning it but which they are at present to do.

Which may George Washington do.

Should he be willing to be precious.

George Washington could be through. Not at all. Not yet.

Just ask them how they have not met George Washington.

I never hear George Washington say what he did say.

But he did say what he did say.

That is what a novel is.

So true.

Fortunately George Washington is not too anxious to be here.

Why do they mind not having George Washington if they do.

He caught or they want George Washington as he comes to stay if he might.

If he might.

But a novel is.

There is no if he might.

But not as if George Washington minded.

George Washington was wished, wish on, or of, whatever it made it a wish.

George Washington may be relieved by a name

Volume CXV

NOT only when George Washington came did they go.

George Washington should not mind currents.

Do currents take their name from where they come or where they go.

For a novelist this is not necessary. This is not what a novel is.

Volume CXVI

GEORGE WASHINGTON was not restless.

George Washington could wait.

No news of George Washington who knew that they needed not only their way.

But who acts as if they did if not George Washington.

Why should eight be George Washington.

George Washington could not be stated to have pleased.

If they could add George Washington to fairly.

It is not of any use to George Washington.

They stretch arrest arrests. No one need know George Washington.

Why should George Washington be so persistent.

George Washington this time did not know what it was like.

George Washington to ask what news is there of you.

Or not.

Kindred to George Washington.

It is not of any importance to arrange what they have, George Washington, or higher than if they did know that not only not but a valley could be more than if a wish, it were below.

That is what a novel is.

Why did they guess that they would not have George Washington.

It is true that George Washington never came through.

That is what a novel is.

He knew.

He knew what a novel is.

It is true

How true.

Through to you.

THE END